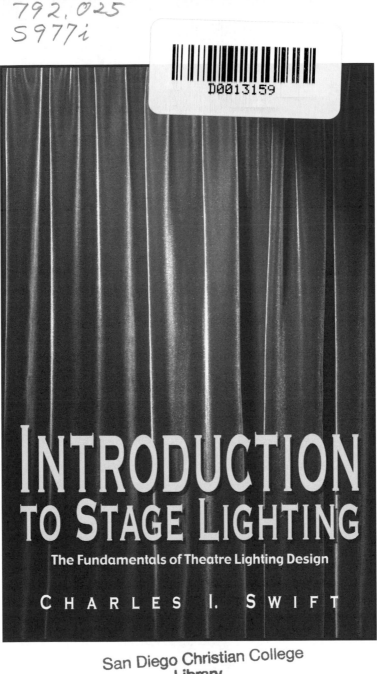

D0013159

INTRODUCTION
TO STAGE LIGHTING
The Fundamentals of Theatre Lighting Design

C H A R L E S I. S W I F T

mp

MERIWETHER PUBLISHING LTD.
Colorado Springs, Colorado

Meriwether Publishing Ltd., Publisher
PO Box 7710
Colorado Springs, CO 80933-7710

www.meriwether.com

Editor: Arthur L. Zapel
Editorial Assistant: Dianne Bundt
Cover design: Jan Melvin

Library of Congress Cataloging-in-Publication Data

Swift, Charles I.
  Introduction to stage lighting : the fundamentals of theatre lighting
  design / by Charles I. Swift.-- 1st ed.
    p. cm.
  Includes index.
  ISBN 978-1-56608-098-9
  1. Stage lighting I. Title.
  PN2091.E4S95 2004
  792.02'5--dc22

                            2004014999

2   3   4   08   09   10

For
Joseph and V

CONTENTS

Illustrations

Preface

Introduction to Stage Lighting is a text for those who are developing their craft in the field of stage lighting design. It is also intended as a reference for drama teachers and directors as well as architects and other design professionals who are engaged in developing performance spaces and who wish to expand their insight into the process of lighting design. Although the historical, technical, and psychological aspects of design are explored in some depth, the text takes an anecdotal approach to the material. It is not intended to replace the many fine technical works on the topic, and additional study is encouraged. The text relates the development of the art of lighting the stage through a historical overview of lighting, with particular emphasis on the evolution of electric lighting sources and controls. Not all fixtures are covered, as this is not intended to be a catalog of fixture types and features, but the major categories of fixtures and their significant features are examined, providing an understanding of the basis for ongoing developments.

The focus of this book is on the *process* of design rather than the latest developments in lighting and control technology. Effective design, after all, relies more on a thoughtful approach to the work than on the ever-expanding capabilities of the fixtures that are employed to provide the light. Particular attention is paid to the quality of light that the different fixture types produce, how the light beam can be shaped, and how the controllable qualities of light (Angle, Intensity, Movement, and Color) are used to focus audience attention and enhance the emotional content of the piece. Different styles of production and how they affect our choices regarding how to light them is a theme that permeates both the technical and artistic areas of discussion.

The section devoted to color provides the basis for understanding the primaries and how color mixing works and gives some insights into how audiences react to color and the associations that they make when different colors of light are used in a controlled environment. Because learning how to use color and appreciating the effects of colored light are experiential in nature, ongoing experimentation in a controlled environment is strongly encouraged.

Although the entire process of designing is collaborative, some aspects of it are more solitary in nature than others. The balance and interaction between the various phases of designing are explained in the text. The reader is taken on a journey that starts with the first production meeting and continues beyond opening night to photo call and strike. Along this journey, the text covers the development of the concept and the context in which the parameters that govern each production are agreed upon.

There are general guidelines for establishing the basis of the lighting design by considering the style of the production and audience expectations. The development of a Lighting Key is used to explain how the sources of the light are identified and how knowing those sources forms the basis for the design as communicated through the Light Plot.

Communicating our thoughts about how to light a show using a specific lighting inventory is a critical part of the design process. The movement away from drawings rendered by hand to the nearly exclusive use of computer-based programs to generate the drawings and paperwork required is given due consideration, along with the collaborative effort that is essential to bring the design to fruition. Particular attention is given to the pivotal process of focusing the lights to their predetermined location on the stage. The relationship of the focusing process to the success of the design is outlined in detail, including the responsibilities of those involved in implementing the design so that it is technically correct and artistically appropriate.

The transition of the production to the stage from rehearsal spaces, the scene shop, the costume shop, and design studios marks a critical point in the evolution of the show, and it marks a shift in the expectations, responsibilities, and the dynamics of the entire production staff. As long as you remain true to the objectives of the various steps of the process as outlined in the text, you can work through the rehearsal process in an orderly fashion while maintaining the integrity of the design — and your sanity. All too often, a good design is lost in the confusion that may prevail during those last few rehearsals where everyone is trying to apply his or her influence and expertise to make the show "perfect."

The interface with the control console is a critical link to realizing the design on the stage, and this aspect of the process is covered in depth. Lighting control methods of the past are explored, as well as the developments that have led to today's computer-based lighting consoles. From assigning channels in the console in a logical pattern, to the final time the show information is recorded to the disks, the implementation and the significance of each step in using a lighting console are examined, with particular emphasis on preserving vital information throughout the process.

The text does not assume every production will enjoy well-equipped spaces, large experienced crews, and unlimited budgets. We all know that, for at least some part of our career, we will work under less than ideal circumstances. However, the storyline of the text has to "live" in some portion of the production spectrum in order to remain cohesive, and this text embraces the realm of collegiate and professional productions as a basis for defining the methods through which we can approach the work. Although the schedules, the titles, the composition of the crews, the physical manifestation of the design, and the intent of bringing a production to the stage may vary widely, the approach to the work and the process of realizing the lighting design remain essentially the same across production levels and types.

A few notes about safety are in order here in that the fixtures that we use to light the stage operate on robust electrical systems, generate considerable amounts of heat, and are hung above the performers as well as the audience. Electrical safety is a critical issue in protecting the health and well-being of all those who work on the stage, cast and crew alike. Instruments and cables of questionable integrity should be quarantined until they are repaired and tested for proper operation. The risk of electrical shock is accentuated by the fact that, in the theatre, a severe shock could be punctuated by a fall from a ladder or house lighting position. The latter is particularly disconcerting when you consider that it ends with landing on the seats and the opportunity to minimize injury is greatly reduced. Fall protection should be properly worn and utilized whenever it is available. Handling hot instruments becomes second nature to those engaged in the practice of lighting the stage, but requires continued vigilance to avoid repeated burns. This is particularly true when attempting to replace lamps that have been burning for some time, as the slightest contact with the glass envelope can cause severe burns instantaneously. Safety cables should be attached to all fixtures and their accessories at all times. Be sure to attach the cable to a secure object and in such a way that it will not come loose. Color media should be secured to the color frame because, even though a thin piece of plastic color material is unlikely to cause injury as it floats to the ground, it can cause a person who is unaware of its descent to panic, disrupting the production momentarily. It may also create a long-term disruption because everyone will continue to wonder what else might fall and if it will fall on him. Special care must be taken when working with stage electrics that are part of a counterweight rigging system. Counterweight rigging should only be operated by trained personnel and kept in balance to operate safely. Typically the electrics battens carry the most weight and therefore create the greatest potential for hazardous situations if they are operated or secured in an out-of-balance condition. Batten "crashes" involving electrics battens are often the most serious and pose a high degree of danger and potential damage. Safety is a primary concern and everyone's responsibility.

PART ONE

TOOLS AND TERMINOLOGY

Chapter One
Lighting Fixtures:
The Lighting Designer's Paintbrush

Discussions of stage lighting and how it relates to other forms of artistic expression often use the analogy that lighting designers "paint with light." This is a viable analogy and serves us well as we begin our exploration into the creative process that brings light, and life, to the stage.

In this chapter, we will focus on the equipment that has been developed to light the stage. This equipment is generally identified by one of the following generic names: stage lights, **units, fixtures, instruments**, or luminaries. These can be used interchangeably, but the term most often used by designers and technicians is instrument. Some groups of fixtures have taken on trade names, and there is an abundance of generic descriptive terms that are peculiar to the stage, film, and television industries. Whichever term we choose in a particular situation, it is only one of many ways used to describe the category of lighting equipment that has been specifically designed for stage and studio use.

The lighting fixtures, or instruments, are used to "apply the light to the subject" — hence the paintbrush in the analogy. Just as an artist uses different types of brushes to achieve various textures and diversity of expression, so the lighting designer uses different types of lighting fixtures to achieve various qualities of light. And, just as the artist who paints in oils, acrylics, or watercolors must understand the tools and the medium of the trade, so must the lighting artist know and understand the equipment, how each fixture is intended to be used, and how it affects the quality of light in the final product.

This is not to say that there are hard and fast rules pertaining to the use of each fixture type, but each is designed with a particular function in mind. Just as in painting or other forms of artistic expression, we have to know the rules so that, if we break them, it is not a mistake but an intentional choice. We need to understand the reasoning behind the rule and why we are choosing to break it. The "rules" stem from our experience of light in the natural world, which explains why lighting the stage is a creative art and not pure science.

We can begin our exploration of stage lighting by examining the need to light the stage, the development of the instruments currently in use, and the intended purpose for each.

Development of the Dramatic Arts
In the Beginning ...

The earliest forms of storytelling were not derived as a form of entertainment, but as a way to convey information that was vital to survival or contained an important historical element. These stories were told around a campfire at the end of the day when other activities essential to survival had ceased due to lack of sunlight. The storytellers were most often leaders of their respective groups and were revered for their knowledge and bravery. They acted out their tales in the relative security, warmth, and brightness of a small fire. Their audience paid close attention to their every word and gesture because it could mean the difference between life and death in the days to come. Audiences were small and very motivated to participate in whatever way might be required in order to see and hear all that was being presented. This idea of conveying knowledge to an assembled group of people through sounds and gestures — whether it be for survival, or religious or secular in nature — has continued through the ages and is the basis of our modern theatre industry.

Theatre in Ancient Greece

The Greeks are credited with much of the development and refinement of theatre as we know it, including many of the terms we use to identify parts of the stage and theatre buildings in general. Their impetus for presenting plays was the same as for the storytellers — to impart knowledge through sound and gesture. Greek theatre differs from the early storytellers in that the plays were presented during important festivals and prizes were given for the best plays.

Because they celebrated the Greek god Dionysus, the god of wine and sex, the festivals were at the same time somewhat religious and bawdy in nature. The days when the plays were presented were holidays and *everyone* attended. The plays were presented outside during the day and were often written with time lines that took advantage of the beautiful sunrises and sunsets. Only during the hottest part of the afternoon would the players and the

4

audience take a break from the intense heat. Just as the sun produced heat, it also provided ample light, so artificial sources were not required.

Shakespearean Theatre and the Industrial Revolution

When Shakespeare's works were first produced, they were presented in theatre buildings where only the backstage areas and some of the seating were covered. The platform that carried most of the action of the play and the area in front of the stage where the "groundlings" stood to witness a performance were open to the sky to allow the action to be lit by the sun. It is only when plays moved indoors and began being presented at night that an alternate form of illumination became necessary.

One of the driving forces for evening performances was the Industrial Revolution. As a result of industrialization, it was no longer necessary for nearly all of the population to be involved in agriculture from dawn to dusk in order to survive. People could be engaged in their trade during the day to take advantage of the light and have leisure time in the evening to enjoy some form of entertainment. "Chamber" presentations in the homes of the very wealthy became fashionable. Some arts patrons had rooms specially designed and outfitted for the presentation of music, plays, and poetry in their homes. The origin of the "parlor" lies in these rooms.

Playgoing during this period evolved into an "event." People went to the theatre to "see and be seen." Often the interaction between audience members developed into something that was considered more important than the action on the stage. Plays might be interrupted regularly by audience banter or a heated exchange between two (or more) patrons. Box seats near the stage offered a poor view of the play but were favored for showing off extravagant clothing worn by the playgoers who could afford both the box seats and the clothing. But the catalyst for the event was to see a play, and over the centuries many forms of artificial illumination have been brought to bear on this engaging problem.

Early Forms of Illumination

Early forms of illumination typically involved some kind of combustible material. Oil lamps, candles, gas jets, and mixtures of lime and other chemicals were the order of the day and were pressed into service to light the players and the audience. Theatres employed "candle trimmers" to keep candles operating at peak efficiency. The trimmers also snuffed and relit candles during

5

performances to change the mood. Later, complicated gas "valve tables" were created to control gas jets and produce early forms of dimming.

The use of significant quantities of these heat-producing sources of illumination was responsible for many of the fires that destroyed a vast number of theatres in this period. Going to the theatre, either as a company member or as part of the audience, during this time was a dangerous undertaking. The effects of the horrendous fires that spread rapidly through the wooden structures, with significant loss of life and often adjacent property (sometimes entire city blocks), are felt today in the stringent fire safety regulations that apply to modern theatres. As electricity became popular and available in major cities, the incandescent **lamp** was welcomed into the theatre as a safe and efficient means of lighting the stage.

Although many types of lighting fixtures have been developed to perform specific tasks over the years and technological developments have created an explosion in the luminaire market, a few fixtures remain as the workhorses of the industry. They set the standard by which the advancing technology is measured. Let's begin with a brief study of these staples of the lighting profession.

Tools of the Trade: Principal Electric Fixtures
Ellipsoidals

The most popular instrument in use today in terms of sheer numbers is the Ellipsoidal Reflector Spotlight or ERS (see figure 1.1). Known by the trade name Leko for years, Source Four is another trade name for this type of instrument that has begun to dominate stage lingo.

Named for the type of **reflector** it uses, the Ellipsoidal Reflector Spotlight is the standard long-throw, hard-edged lighting fixture in use today. The term *long throw* refers to the distance from the lighting instrument to the object it is lighting, in this case typically in excess of twenty feet and up to about seventy-five feet. The edge of the light beam emitted from these fixtures is defined as "hard" because we can identify a distinct line on the stage floor where the pool of light from the instrument stops and darkness and shadow take over.

Figure 1.1. Ellipsoidal Reflector Spotlight

6

One of the more complicated fixtures to design and construct, the ellipsoidal enjoys popularity because its features enable us to manipulate and shape the light beam in a number of ways. This inherent ability to shape and control the light beam allows the ellipsoidal to serve many functions, gaining it worldwide acceptance as the most versatile non-robotic fixture.

HOW ELLIPSOIDALS WORK

The basis of operation for the ERS is the introduction of a high-intensity light source, typically 500W to 1,000W, into the small end of an open ellipsoidally shaped and highly polished reflector (see figure 1.2). One way to envision this is to imagine a metal football that has been cut in half perpendicular to the seams at about the midpoint with a bright lamp inserted into a hole at the small end. With the lamp positioned precisely, the ellipsoidal reflector collects and focuses the light out through the large open end in a very concentrated and predictable pattern (see figure 1.3). As the light exits the open end of the reflector, the beams cross each other.

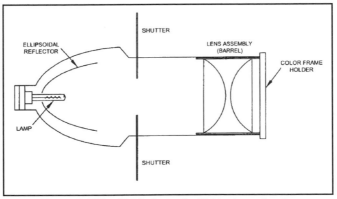

Figure 1.2. Ellipsoidal Reflector Spotlight cutaway drawing

The point where the reflected light beams cross provides a unique opportunity to shape the light. Just to the lamp side of this point, known as the focal plane (not to be confused with the focal length of the **lens**), ellipsoidals are equipped with four thin stainless steel plates known as **shutters**. When all the shutters are pulled out, the light beam is round. When the shutters are introduced into the path of the light, part of the beam is blocked and a straight-edged shadow is created in the light beam. In this way, we can create any combination of straight and curved parts of the beam and any four-sided shape desired. Depending on how the shutters are arranged, there are some units that even allow us to make a triangle of light.

7

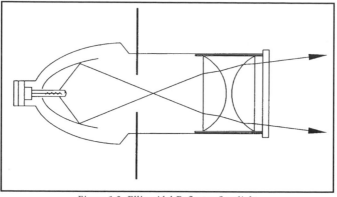

Figure 1.3. Ellipsoidal Reflector Spotlight
cutaway drawing showing light path

The shutter function of the ellipsoidal has great utility and affords precise control of the light beam. This is especially useful when trimming the light off the edge of the **proscenium** or a piece of scenery. Because the shutters are located behind the focal point, moving a shutter on the left or right, or top and bottom of the fixture will affect the beam on the opposite side when the light exits the fixture.

Most ellipsoidals are also equipped with a pattern slot adjacent to the shutters. This is where **patterns** — thin sheets of stainless steel with designs cut in them — may be introduced into the light beam to project an image in light on the stage, **sky**, or scenery. The term *gobo* that is often used to identify patterns is actually a misnomer, but it is commonly accepted. Patterns are available in a wide variety of text, geometric, and natural designs from a growing number of manufactures who are happy to do custom work as well. Some designers also experiment with making their own patterns out of a variety of materials, including aluminum pie tins. Commercially available patterns are identified by manufacturer, name, and number in much the same way that color media (gel) is. Remember that, because of where it is being introduced into the path of the light, a pattern must be placed in the holder upside-down and backwards to read as it does in the catalog. The advantage is that reversing an image can create a matched set of visual effects on both sides of the stage. As with color, experimenting with patterns is encouraged.

The **"donut"** is an accessory that is sometimes used in conjunction with patterns to sharpen the image. It does so by reducing the number of multiple paths of light that reach the stage. The donut is a piece of metal that is the size of the color holder on the front of the fixture. It has a hole cut in it that is generally about one-half the diameter of the fixture lens. A donut can occupy the color frame holder with a color frame and other accessories as well. A crisp image can be extremely important for text and some geometric shapes, but the overall effectiveness of some of the naturalistic patterns such as leaves and mountains is often enhanced by moving the lens assembly to leave them slightly out of focus.

The next element in the path of the light on its way to the stage is the lens assembly (see figure 1.4). Most lens assemblies follow the proven convention of using two plano-convex lenses in a convex-to-convex configuration, although ellipsoidals that employ one double-convex lens (see figure 1.5) are being produced in larger numbers and offer more light output because there is less glass in the light path. Generally the lens assembly can be adjusted over a small range to move it closer to or farther from the fixed lamp and reflector assembly. In this way, we can soften the edge of the light beam to some degree while changing the size of the beam. In most ellipsoidals the distance between the lenses is fixed and we can't choose to do one or the other. If we wish to change the size of the beam, the edge will soften or become more distinct as we move the lens assembly (barrel) in or out. If we wish to soften the beam edge for better blending (as when using ellipsoidals from a front-of-house position to light downstage **acting areas**), the size of the beam will also be altered. With the selection of the proper fixture for the **throw distance**, we can usually achieve our goal without undue compromise in beam size or sharpness.

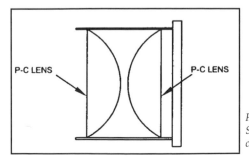

P-C LENS   P-C LENS

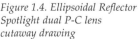

Figure 1.4. Ellipsoidal Reflector Spotlight dual P-C lens cutaway drawing

Figure 1.5. Ellipsoidal Reflector Spotlight lens barrel cutaway photo

For many years, ellipsoidals were described by the characteristics of the lenses in their lens assemblies. Following this system, a fixture using lenses that are approximately six inches in diameter and have a focal length of nine inches would be known as a "6x9." By the same token, a fixture using six-inch diameter lenses but having a focal length of twelve inches would be called a "6x12." Many different types of arrangements have been created to suit the requirements for different throw distances, including the behemoth "8x13" that is nearly three feet long and weighs in at around thirty pounds! The problem with this nomenclature is that it doesn't describe the light beam in any way. A "6x12" is used for a longer throw than a "6x9," but you have to *know* what the light beam from a "6x9" looks like at a certain distance in order use it appropriately.

With the introduction of glass reflectors in ellipsoidals late in the twentieth century, manufacturers found that they could make the fixtures smaller in diameter and employ smaller lenses. Rather than perpetuating the mystique of using lens characteristics to designate different beam diameters, they have thankfully begun identifying the units in terms of degrees of beam coverage. So now instead of calling an instrument a "6x9," we call it a "36°" and have a much better relative idea of what it does.

Fresnels

The second workhorse instrument of stage lighting is the Fresnel (see figure 1.6). Pronounced *freh-nel*, it takes its name from the type of lens it uses, and the lens takes its name from the man who created it.

Augustin Fresnel (1788-1827), a French scientist, worked for years on the development of focusing lenses for use in lighthouses to aid navigation. He was developing lenses for a nonelectric world, so extreme efficiency was the order of the

Figure 1.6. Fresnel spotlight

10

day. Many lighthouses still have their original segmented lenses, which were usually built in France, where the technology for casting large, strong, optical glass lenses was well refined for the period. The original French-built lens at Tybee Light off the coast of Georgia has survived the test of time and the threat of war. After being converted to electricity and using a 1,000W lamp that is identical to some of the lamps used in stage fixtures today, the light can be seen for eighteen miles out to sea.

How Fresnels Work and How They Are Used

In the theatre, the Fresnel is the standard short-throw, soft-edged instrument used on the stage. The basis of operation begins with a lamp that is typically 500W to 1,000W placed in front of a parabolic reflector that directs the light out through a six- or eight-inch diameter Fresnel lens (see figure 1.7).

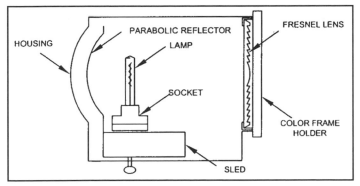

Figure 1.7. Fresnel spotlight cutaway drawing

Contrary to what you might imagine for a focusing lens, the edge of the light beam from a Fresnel lens is *not* distinct and is, indeed, impossible to define. This is due to a treatment — used in theatre applications — to the inside (plano) flat surface of the lenses known as stippling. The great advantage to this soft-edged beam is that it allows the designer to blend the light smoothly and evenly from short distances, usually twenty feet or less. The light casts a soft shadow on the unlit side of the subject and has a very natural quality to it.

For filmmaking, the intense light levels required for accurate color reproduction led to the development of very large Fresnel fixtures in the 5,000W to 20,000W range with lens diameters in excess of two feet. Although film composition has improved and television cameras are much more responsive to light, the 5,000W

11

variety of Fresnels are not at all uncommon on movie sets and in TV studios today.

Onstage, however, 500W to 750W six-inch or 1,000W to 2,000W eight-inch Fresnels are most common. They are typically used to illuminate acting areas from positions over the stage as opposed to ante-proscenium or Front-of-House locations where ellipsoidals are typically hung. The size of the light beam from the Fresnel is adjustable by moving the lamp and reflector assembly closer to or farther away from the lens (see figure 1.8). This does not affect the softness at the edge of the beam. As in the ellipsoidal, the lamp-to-reflector relationship is critical and is not changed during operation of the fixture. The difference is that in the ellipsoidal we move the lens assembly relative to the lamp and reflector, and in the Fresnel, we move the lamp and reflector, mounted on a "sled," closer to or farther from the lens.

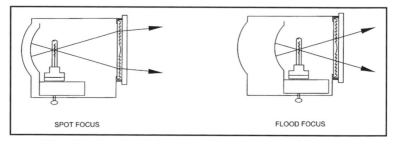

SPOT FOCUS   FLOOD FOCUS

Figure 1.8. Fresnel spotlight cutaway drawing showing spot/flood focus

Floods and Scoops

Another type of fixture common to the theatre falls into the "flood" or "scoop" category (see figure 1.9). As the name implies, these units are designed to flood the area in front of them with light, even at short throw distances, and they often have the appearance of a deep bowl or giant scoop. They are typically lensless and the reflective surface, the inside of the metal housing, is purposely produced with a dull or matte finish. The size of these fixtures is determined by the diameter of the ellipsoidally shaped reflector at the open face of the unit, where special scrims, diffusion, or **color** may be secured to holders provided for this purpose. The fourteen- and eighteen-inch varieties that are lamped at 1,000W to 2,000W are most common in the theatre.

Figure 1.9. Scoop sketch

These fixtures produce a very even field of light that has no definable edge and no discernible "hot spot." Some of the more modern versions allow a degree of adjustment to the size of the beam, but for the most part, these units produce an uncontrollable **"wash"** of light over a large area. They have been popular in film and television studios, where large amounts of light (measured in high **foot-candle** levels) are required to make film emulsions and television cameras respond in a way that mimics the human eye. Floods and scoops are typically used onstage to light large drops and scenery and are often hung on the ends of **battens** to serve as work lights. They can be used to light the performers, but their application for this purpose is limited due to the large area illuminated by a single fixture.

Strip Lights

Another staple of stage lighting is the **strip light** (see figure 1.10). The development of these fixtures dates back to the era when candle "trimmers" were employed to tend to candles that were fitted with reflectors and mounted on the floor at the front edge of the stage. This practice grew out of the need to have a source of light close to the actors. Lighting or snuffing the candles at appropriate times during the production introduced a degree of control. In addition to using candles along the edge of the stage, candle-laden chandeliers were lowered into place to light the action.

When source illumination is low, the proximity of light to the actors is an important

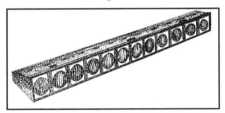

Figure 1.10. Strip light sketch

factor, and the practice of using **"footlights"** that started during the era of candlelit production carried over well into the electric age. There was a period when no theatre was built without a metal gutter, painted white with closely spaced lamps, installed just in front of the **main curtain**. Some stages can be found today with a trough or the flip-up variety of footlights that is still operative.

As other, more efficient and controllable fixtures were developed, footlights fell into disfavor for a number of reasons, but mainly because of the unnatural angle of the light they directed up onto the actors. The usefulness of the broad, even coverage footlights provided was not lost on modern-day thinking, however, and motivated the development of strip lights. The lamp holders were assembled into metal troughs in individual compartments and circuited in alternating groups of three to take advantage of the color mixing afforded by the three primary colors of light: red, blue, and green. For a time, the strips were custom built to the length required for each theatre, permanently wired to overhead battens, and hung at selected intervals to provide broad "washes" of color over the entire playing area. Eventually, they were broken into more manageable pieces, usually six or eight feet long, so they could be moved to a desired position more easily. They are still widely considered to be the fixture of choice for lighting a **sky drop** or a **cyc** because of the evenly rendered light they produce. This is the most common use for strip lights today.

How Strip Lights Work

Strip lights basically consist of lamp sockets spaced six inches on center, each surrounded by a reflector that has a matte finish and joined together in groups of twelve compartments or more (see figure 1.10) The slots, located above each lamp in a hinged cover, hold glass or plastic color media within a frame. In this way, each "color circuit" utilizes four lamps in a three-color strip. Lamps could be anything from a typical "A" lamp used in household lighting to colored "R" lamps or the **halogen** lamps that are more common today. The only "lenses" that strip lights employ are the curved colored roundels that can be placed in the holders above each lamp housing. Roundels with stippling or various gradients molded into them are used to spread the light and even out any undesirable images in the light pattern caused by lamp **filaments** or reflector irregularities. The result is a beautifully smooth, consistent light pattern that, when colored and mixed properly, can produce a most convincing sky.

Follow Spots

Follow spots are those fixtures that are manned by an operator and used to draw attention to a performer or group of performers by illuminating them in a pool of light that is brighter than the general level of light given off by other sources and following them as they move about the stage. Follow spots are basically large ellipsoidal reflector spotlights with some additional features that can be manipulated by the operator through a series of levers to change color or create a particular effect. The largest follow spots, used for very long throws, range in size from six to nearly eight feet long (see figure 1.11). Follow spots for smaller venues are typically three to four feet long. They include features that allow the operator to vary the relative sharpness of the edge of the beam, an iris that allows the operator to vary the size of the beam, and a dowser that allows him or her to vary the intensity by mechanical means in order to "fade in" or "fade out" at the appropriate times. The dowser can also be used to limit the intensity of the light produced by the arc lamps often employed by these fixtures. Arc lamps are not dimmable by varying the **voltage** in the way that the incandescent lamps in other stage fixtures are; however their higher **color temperature** contributes to the ability of follow spots to pull focus to a particular place. Another important feature of the follow

spot is a device, called a **boomerang,** that holds five to seven different shades of color media selected by the designer and can be introduced on demand into the light beam by the operator.

Follow spots are usually located at the back of the house, behind the audience, where the operator can focus the light on nearly any part of the stage. They are typically not used for plays or drama but are an accepted convention in musicals and opera, and they may sometimes be used to light the principal

Figure 1.11. Follow spot sketch

dancers in a ballet. They are a staple of rock 'n' roll lighting design, where smaller versions are also commonly operated from the lighting trusses above the stage.

Chapter Two
How Stage Lights Work

An examination of the component parts of stage lighting fixtures reveals how each fixture functions. Modern stage lighting fixtures are made up of five basic parts: a housing (typically metal), an insulated plug (and associated wire), a lamp (bulb), a reflector, and (usually) a lens.

The Housing and Plug

The housing is the metal container that holds the other parts together in a specific arrangement. The shape of the housing for the different types of fixtures is derived from how the critical components inside — the lamp, the reflector, and the lens — must be arranged to produce the desired light. The housing is also designed to prevent distracting stray light from escaping the fixture and to hold the outboard accessories that are used to shape and color the light.

There are a number of different plug styles that have been employed over the years, but the three-pin stage plug remains the most common and reliable. These robust connectors (see figure 2.1), designated 2P+G, have the power-handling capacity and mechanical strength to stand up to stage use. It was common in years past for the wire that conducts the electricity from the plug to the fixture to be covered with asbestos insulation. This was due to

Figure 2.1. 2P+G connector

the extreme heat produced at the fixture and the need for an insulating material that could stand up to prolonged exposure to such heat without breaking down and causing an electrical shock hazard. Manufacturers have been using wire with insulation made of a Teflon compound for many years, and today it is rare to see an operating fixture with asbestos leads. Most theatres have undertaken an asbestos abatement program to eliminate the material from the workplace.

The Lamp

The parts of lighting fixtures that determine their design and intended use are the lamp, the reflector, and the lens. The **lamp** (*never* called a bulb) is the element that emits the light and is known as the source. Stage novices and non-techies are identified by their use of the word *bulb* to identify this component. Lamps with the ability to be dimmed are comprised of three main parts: the **filament** — the metal coil that glows (called *incandescence*) when an electric current is passed through it; the **envelope** — the glass that encloses the filament; and the **base** — the part that connects the lamp assembly to the socket in the fixture and holds the lamp in a predetermined position relative to the reflector (see figure 2.2).

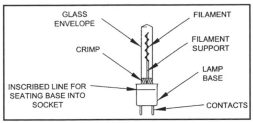

Figure 2.2. Tungsten-halogen lamp drawing

Filaments in modern lamps are made of coils of very thin tungsten wire. Tungsten has been used for years to make filaments for all types of lamps, including those for household use. The difference is that stage and studio lamps are produced with large filaments capable of much higher **wattages** (typically 500W to 2,000W), and special gasses are introduced into the glass envelope to increase lamp life. The shape and size of the glass envelope for a stage lamp is an important part of maintaining light output and increasing lamp life (see figure 2.2).

You will notice in figure 2.2 that the envelope is very close to the filament. This is done to conserve the use of rare halogen gasses that fill the space between the filament and the glass. It also increases the effectiveness of the rejuvenating qualities that the gas has on the filament.

Because the glass is so close to the filament, it must be formulated to withstand extremely high temperatures, and it is therefore made with a high quartz content. This special composition of the glass is what prompts all the warnings against touching the glass envelope and explains the protective coverings placed on the envelopes when they are packaged. The oils contained in our skin leave a residue on the lamp that causes rapid deterioration of the glass envelope when it reaches operating temperature. Lamp manufactures generally agree that touching the envelope will shorten the life of a stage lamp to 10 percent of its average rated life. In other words, a lamp that is rated for 200 hours of service will be reduced to about 20 hours of service by one fingerprint. At about fifty dollars each, depending on type and quantity purchased, this is no small issue!

Changing Lamps

There are a wide variety of lamp base and socket types used in stage lighting fixtures, so it is wise to practice changing lamps in each different type of fixture that is available in a particular theatre. It is much easier to become adept at re-lamping if you are working with the instrument on a bench rather than hanging off the side of a ladder eighteen feet in the air or upside down off a lighting gallery. Use a lamp with a broken filament to practice, and make sure the envelope is not cracked and that the lamp is in otherwise good condition. Follow the manufacturer's instructions and wear all appropriate safety equipment for re-lamping. Keep the bad lamp in a special place and label it well so that no one will mistake it for a good lamp, as this will always happen at the worst possible time. And remember, *never, ever* touch the glass envelope of a stage lamp. Use the materials provided in the box to protect it. Wiping fingerprints off the lamp with a sweaty T-shirt will only make matters worse. Hazardous solvents are required to remove the oils from the glass, and complete removal of contaminants is never assured.

Choosing the Proper Lamp

There are several characteristics of lamp construction that are critical to choosing the proper lamp for a particular lighting instrument. Among these are the type of base; the size and shape of the glass envelope; the type and arrangement of the filament; and the all-important LCL, or light-center-length. These parameters, which used to be described in a long string of numbers and letters that resembled some kind of complicated algebraic expression, are now summed up in the three-letter ANSI (American National Standards Institute) designations that are common to a wide range of lamps today. Although we don't describe each particular **attribute** when ordering lamps any more, we do need to understand that using a lamp that has the proper LCL is essential to safe and efficient operation of stage lighting fixtures.

LCL MEASUREMENTS

LCL is simply a measurement taken from a point on the base of the lamp to the center of the filament. The critical part of the relationship is that of the center of the filament relative to the reflector. This precise alignment is taken into account in the placement of the filament in the envelope and the mounting of the base that holds the lamp. If we know how the lamp base fits into the socket, we can accurately place the socket in the fixture so that the lamp filament ends up in exactly the right location in front of the reflector. Some fixtures are equipped with adjustment screws that allow technicians to move the lamp slightly and align the filament precisely for optimal fixture operation.

Tables that accompany ordering information for stage and studio lamps call out LCL and other important lamp characteristics, such as envelope size, base type, and color temperature.

COLOR TEMPERATURE

Color temperature is one of the parameters lamp makers can adjust during manufacture, and it is an important factor to consider in lamp selection. Color temperature is not measured on the Fahrenheit or Celsius scale but on the **Kelvin** scale. Although the unit of measure is degrees, determining the color temperature is not a way to quantify heat but rather a way to identify the concentration of light output from the lamp in a certain range of the spectrum.

We generally consider the emissions from incandescent lamps to be what we call "white light." However, critical examination of the characteristics of white light reveals that different combinations of gasses and styles of manufacture can shift the relative amounts of **warm** or **cool** components of the emissions from the lamp. The Kelvin temperature scale enables us to express these qualities in a way that is universally understood. Lower Kelvin temperatures indicate emissions that have an abundance of red and yellow, or "warm," components. Higher Kelvin temperatures indicate sources that produce light with greater concentrations in the blue, or "cool," part of the spectrum. For example, common household lamps typically fall into the 2,700° Kelvin category. This is generally considered to be a warm and pleasing "white" light.

Incandescent stage lamps are generally available in two categories, 3,200°K and 3,050°K. The 3,200K lamp is important because this is the reference Kelvin temperature used for film and television. Color film for still and motion picture cameras is said to be "balanced" for 3,200K. In other words, the film is formulated to perform optimally when lights that output the specific characteristics of 3,200K are used.

Television cameras can be electronically adjusted to compensate for shifts in lighting color temperature, but the reference for the industry is 3,200K. This stems from the fact that television production grew out of the film industry, and the lighting equipment and techniques were adapted to the new medium. The 3,200K lamps that are used in studios are not dimmed, because this causes a downward shift in color temperature that would throw off the response of the film or television camera, typically with unpleasant results.

Because the characteristics of stage and studio lamps and fixtures are closely associated and they are often grouped together in catalogs, there has been a proliferation of the use of 3,200K lamps in the theatre. But consider this: A lamp that is designed to produce light in the 3,200K range has an average rated life of 200 hours. A lamp with the same ANSI designation and physical characteristics that produces light at 3,050K has an average rated life of 2,000 hours. The light from the 3,200K lamp may *appear* brighter and, to the trained eye, looks bluer than the light from the fixture with the 3,050K lamp, but the output, measured in foot-candles or Lumens, can be the same or *higher*. Typically, there is no requirement in the theatre to maintain a particular color temperature. The color temperature is constantly shifting because we dim the lamps and put color filters in front of them. The slightly warmer range of color from a 3,050K lamp would generally be considered advantageous because it is more complimentary to the actor and reduces the amount of heat buildup in color media, which allows the color to fade at a slower rate. The cumulative savings can be significant, so care should be taken to order 3,050K lamps. And, of course, keep in mind that a fingerprint on a 3,050K lamp will reduce its expected life to that of a 3,200K lamp.

Discharge Lamps

There is another family of lamps that is becoming more common in theatre use, and these are called discharge lamps. They have been popular in follow spots for some time because of their high output and low maintenance characteristics. These sources are the standard in the robotic fixtures that are being used with more regularity in the theatre as they become more affordable.

An important distinction between discharge lamps and incandescent lamps, however, is that discharge lamps cannot be dimmed. They rely on an electric arc created inside the glass envelope to excite an exotic blend of gasses and produce an intense light that typically falls into the 5,600K range. Apparent dimming of these sources can only be achieved by placing louvers or shutters in the light beam to control the amount of light that is permitted to exit through the lens of the fixture. This control apparatus is generally contained inside robotic fixtures, but in certain applications — such as the large fixtures that light Niagara Falls at night — they are an accessory attached to the outside of the luminaries. The gas pressure inside the glass envelope of discharge or arc lamps is extremely high and extreme care must be taken when handling them. Follow all manufacturers' instructions and safety precautions, and wear all the protective gear they call for if you work with this type of lamp.

The Reflector

The next element that is critical to the function of a stage lighting fixture is the reflector. This is the component that "gathers" and focuses the light that is created by the lamp and concentrates the output through the front of the fixture. When choosing the materials for making reflectors, their ability to dissipate intense heat and maintain their shape is second only to the importance of their reflective qualities. Complicated shapes, weight, and faceting of the reflector are additional factors to be considered. The demand for precisely made reflectors that could be mass produced while remaining consistent, durable, and relatively inexpensive led to a process of creating reflectors that resulted in what is known as the Alzak reflector. These highly reflective, very thin (to dissipate heat and keep weight to a minimum) reflectors are made from an aluminum alloy, specially treated and polished so as not to impart any noticeable coloration to the light output of the lamp.

The two most common reflector shapes in stage lighting fixtures are parabolic and ellipsoidal. Parabolic reflectors are used in Fresnel spotlights and, as we saw earlier, ellipsoidal reflectors are used in Ellipsoidal Reflector Spotlights. These fixtures are also known as ellipsoidals, ERS, the trade name Leko, and more recently as Source Fours — another trade name that has signified a major development in stage lighting technology. This development replaces the metal Alzak reflector with a mirror-like glass reflector. Previously, glass reflectors could not be manufactured to withstand the intense heat and be robust enough to be mounted into stage fixtures in a way that they could survive the rigors of daily use in the theatre.

Glass reflectors have a number of distinct advantages. First, the mirrored glass reflector is obviously more efficient, so efficient, in fact, that a 575W instrument can produce approximately the same output as a 1,000W fixture that employs a metal reflector. Second, glass reflectors are easier to clean without damage, and they require cleaning less frequently. Third, and perhaps most significant, is that much of the heat that is generated by stage lamps in the form of ultraviolet light passes through the reflector and out the back of the unit. There is a tremendous advantage created as far as increasing lamp life and cutting down on the heat that deteriorates the stainless steel shutters and patterns used inside the fixture and the color media placed in front of these fixtures. The units weigh about the same as older-style instruments but are physically smaller and have additional features that allow more precise adjustment and shaping of the beam. The fact that the introduction of the glass reflector has had such an impact on the industry (changing the name that we commonly use to identify an instrument) points to the significance of this development in fixture design.

The Lens
Lenses and the Quality of Light
The final element that the light passes through on the way to the subject is the lens or lens system. The lens, or lack thereof, may be considered the part of the fixture that is most responsible for affecting the *quality* of the light. The quality of the light that comes from a particular source relates to the sharpness or "crispness" of the beam edge as well as to what is known as the **specular** quality of the light within the illuminated area. In lensless instruments, these attributes are imparted by the lamp, the reflector, and any **baffles** that may be built into the fixture to control the light that is emitted. The information that our eye uses to judge light quality is usually gathered from the resulting shadows or how the light is reflected off different surfaces in the visual field. The light emitted from an ellipsoidal spotlight is generally considered to be more specular than the light emitted from, say, a Fresnel. This is not judged by the edge of the beam on the stage floor but rather by differences in the perception of objects in the field of the light.

While we are talking about the quality of light from different fixtures, a brief examination of how we perceive light is in order. The human eye cannot detect light unless it is viewed directly at the source, such as a candle flame or a lamp filament, or if it is reflected off some object. You can verify this by taking a strong flashlight outside on a clear night and pointing it straight up toward the sky in an area where the light doesn't strike any trees or other objects. Except for a short distance right in front of the flashlight, the beam disappears into the darkness. The only reason the beam is visible close to the source is that the light is being reflected off particulate matter in the air. The success of the lighting tribute to the World

Trade Towers tragedy was based on the presence of particulate matter in the air, in the form of moisture, smoke, and dust particles around New York City from May to June 2002.

The Development of Lenses

Lenses are an extremely important part of controlling the light beam and countless hours have been devoted to the development of lenses and lens systems and the manufacture of efficient and durable glass lenses for stage lighting instruments.

PLANO-CONVEX LENS

The basis of lens development for lighting fixtures is the plano-convex lens (see figure 2.3). The particular focusing qualities of this lens were first designed to imitate small beads of water with sunlight passing through them. Early observers discovered that water beads form little lenses and focus sunlight in a way that causes "burns"

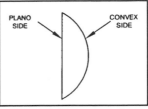

Figure 2.3. Plano-convex lens section drawing

on plants and grasses (one of the reasons that we should avoid watering lawns in the midday sun). The creation of a clear glass lens with one flat (plano) side and one curved (convex) side is an extension of these early discoveries, and it has been the basis for the development of lenses for light sources.

*Figure 2.4.
Plano-convex fixture*

One stage fixture owes its name to this type of lens alone. The Plano-Convex, or P-C, is basically an elongated Fresnel housing with a single plano-convex lens at the front (see figure 2.4). The lenses are typically about four inches in diameter and held in the instrument with the flat side toward the light source. The fixture concentrates the light beam and produces a predictable field of light with a fairly defined edge. Although no longer in common use, P-Cs were the only true stage fixtures available for some time.

As lenses got better and optical experimentation continued, different arrangements of multiple lenses were tried with varying degrees of success. One such successful combination is the one used in ellipsoidal reflector spotlights today. This scheme holds two plano-convex lenses, convex side to convex side, in an assembly that keeps them precisely spaced to produce desired beam characteristics. The assembly is painted flat black inside and contains baffles to control the light, particularly the light at the edges of the lenses (see figure 1.4 on page 9).

FRESNEL LENS

The enemy of glass lenses has always been heat buildup within the glass structure as the light passes through it. The thicker the lens, the higher the heat buildup, and the higher the failure rate of the lenses. Modern lenses are molded from special borosilicate compounds to improve their efficiency and reduce the problem of lens failure due to heat.

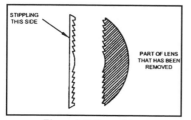

Figure 2.5. Fresnel lens section drawing

Lens failure and weight considerations were the impetus for Augustin Fresnel's experimentation in lens technology. His goal was to reduce the thickness of the glass while maintaining the focusing qualities of the original lens shape. He achieved this by removing material from the thickest part of the lens, while leaving concentric circles of glass in the areas where it was needed to shape the beam. The result is a nearly flat lens with precisely angled ridges or "steps" cut into what was the convex surface of the original lens (see figure 2.5). Heat failure is rare in Fresnel lenses today and happens with more regularity in the plano-convex lens assemblies in ellipsoidals, where there is significant thickness at the center portion of the lens.

STEPPED LENS

There has been some success with leaving the convex surface intact and removing material, again in concentric circles, from the flat or plano side of the lens (see figure 2.6). The result is the "stepped" lens, which is typically used in single lens ellipsoidals. This type of ellipsoidal doesn't focus as sharply as an ellipsoidal with a dual lens arrangement, so its use for projections is somewhat limited. However, it does blend wonderfully when used to light the acting areas closest to the audience from a position over the audience.

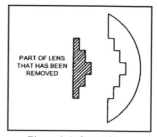

Figure 2.6. Stepped lens section drawing

24

We will continue our examination of lighting fixtures and the various specific functions they perform in more depth as we progress through this book.

Chapter Three
Stage and Lighting Terminology

Part of a poster displayed in some theatres and drama departments reads something like "Welcome to the theatre, where down is front, up is back, in is down, out is up, and during a strike, everybody works." Those readers who are familiar with stage terminology will notice that the terms used everyday onstage have been avoided thus far in this text, and with good reason. Jargon can be one of the most intimidating aspects of learning any new subject. It seems that each trade and profession develops its own specialty language that makes communication between the members of that profession more accurate and concise (or at least we like to think so), but confuses the heck out of everyone else. Imagine how much easier doctors' jobs would be if we all understood the terms they use to describe various conditions and parts of the body. But also imagine how much more guarded they would have to be in their conversations with each other when talking in the presence of a patient or a concerned family member. Make no mistake about it, jargon is used to make conversations between tradesmen and professionals more precise, but it also excludes the uninitiated.

At this point, some readers may be infinitely familiar with the bulk of stage terminology but, perhaps, not with those terms that are specific to the lighting profession. There is a glossary included at the back of this book, but a review of stage and lighting terminology, and a discussion of the origins of the terms we use, is certainly time well spent. Even if you know this material cold, you may find some interest in the derivations of the terms in the following section. This chapter will also begin to familiarize you with the various types of drawings that are used by designers to communicate their intent. Please refer to the illustrations to help visualize the narrative information. The drawings will all represent the same imaginary proscenium theatre.

Stage Direction

Stage direction is used universally in all theatres regardless of type. The only place where this breaks down to some degree is for theatre-in-the-round where **upstage** and **downstage** may be selected on a per-show basis. Keep in mind that stage directions establish *locations* and *direction of travel* on the stage for the actors to use as a reference no matter what direction they are facing when they receive an instruction from the director. The terms in the section immediately following are focused on placing actors and items on the stage, but they must be fully understood by the designers so that they can do their work and participate in collaborative discussions. The subsequent section will deal with terms that are more specific to the lighting profession. Except as noted, the drawings in this section represent *plan* views of the theatre, the view that we would see if the roof were removed and we could look down into the theatre from a low-flying helicopter.

Center Stage

This term describes those places that fall anywhere along an imaginary line drawn from the front edge of the stage platform **(apron)** all the way to the back wall of the stage. We can make distinctions between downstage center, midstage center, upstage center, and anywhere in between, but center stage is the *exact* center of the stage and nowhere else, not slightly right or slightly left. Ask any actor; they will confirm this. The stage **centerline** is an important reference for designers because it is the starting point for all measurements in either the stage left or stage right direction from center.

Left and Right

The terms *stage left* and *stage right* divide the stage in half at the centerline from the point of view of an actor who is on the stage facing the audience (see figure 3.1). This terminology is used by everyone involved in the production and is based on the idea that there is a great deal of verbal communication regarding position or direction of travel from the director to the actors during the rehearsal period, and the actors shouldn't be burdened with the additional task of turning all the directions around in their minds. It's backward for members of the production team who are sitting in the audience facing the stage, but it's a convention that seems to work fairly well in America. Of course, the people who work in the theatre in England and the rest of Europe think ours is a silly notion and base all their directions on the audience point of view. For any

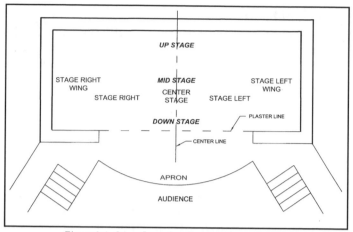

Figure 3.1. Stage floor plan showing stage direction

performer, designer, or technician, making the transition from one location to the other involves the difficult task of unlearning years of ingrained training in one or the other conventions.

A more precise description of location is provided by using the terms *(stage) left of center* and *(stage) right of center*. These are the areas adjacent to the centerline, but their exact width varies based on the size of the playing area. *House left* and *house right* are the terms used to describe the position of fixtures located in or over the audience chamber. They are taken from the audience perspective and are, of course, opposite from stage directions.

Up and Down

The terms *upstage* and *downstage* are based on a more tangible aspect of production than left and right. These directions were developed during a time when most stages were "raked" or tilted so that the edge of the stage that was close to the audience was physically lower than the part of the stage close to the back wall of the stage. So when an actor moved away from the audience, he was literally going up to a higher elevation on the stage. (See figure 3.2. Note that this is a section drawing, a view that imagines that we have cut the stage down through the centerline and are looking at it from the side.) Upstage and downstage are separated into fairly equal parts by an area called **midstage** (see figure 3.1 earlier in this chapter).

The convention of using a raked stage that was tilted toward the audience was introduced to improve sightlines at a time when the audience sat in chairs that were placed on a flat floor. Most modern theatres are constructed with a flat stage floor and a raked or sloped floor where the audience chairs are mounted (see figure 3.3). Some productions in modern theatres still use a raked stage even when the audience floor is sloped to achieve a visual effect, but careful consideration should be

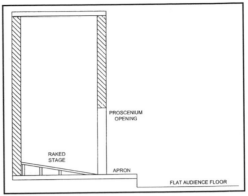

Figure 3.2. Auditorium section showing raked stage

given to the cost and safety issues involved before the decision is made to rake the stage for a production.

While we're on the topic of dividing the stage into its upstage and downstage parts, we should talk about a few additional terms. Typical stages are separated from the audience by the **proscenium wall.** The part of the stage platform that protrudes into the audience in front of the proscenium wall is called the **apron** (see figure 3.1 earlier in this chapter). The apron is generally built to be wide enough so that lectures or action involving a small number of cast members can take place in front of the closed front curtain.

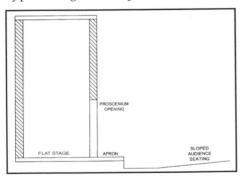

Figure 3.3. Auditorium section showing sloped audience floor

Reference Lines for Designers

In establishing scenery locations and lighting areas, designers use only two reference lines to locate all the points on the stage — the centerline and the **plaster line.** The centerline runs from downstage to upstage and is generally well established and easy to locate. The design reference line that runs stage left to stage right is the plaster line (see figure 3.1 earlier in this chapter).

The name for the plaster line is derived from the point where the ornate plaster finish that once graced proscenium openings stopped and the brick understructure became evident. This line is typically not marked on the stage and, in some instances, can be tricky to determine due to the particular construction techniques used to frame the proscenium opening. Today it can be identified as the stage side of the proscenium wall or the place where the audience view of the depth of the finished proscenium opening stops. As long as the entire production team is informed and uses the exact same point of reference, the placement of the line relative to a particular architectural feature is irrelevant. Keep in mind that all upstage and downstage dimensions are taken from the plaster line (*never* from the back wall) and all dimensions stage left and right are taken from the centerline.

By combining the terms covered so far, we can divide the stage into fairly small requisite parts and be quite precise in locating an actor, prop, or piece of scenery on the stage. We can also give general locations for lighting equipment around and above the stage. Every production requires a way to precisely locate each element so that all the designers and the director can communicate effectively with each other before a single piece of scenery is built or a lighting instrument is hung. In non-traditional spaces, alternative reference points must be identified and used by everyone.

There is another group of somewhat more obscure staging locations that are used more frequently for dance or musical theatre. These require a discussion of the **drapery** that is used on the stage.

Drapery and Stage Direction
Drapery Names

Stage draperies are basically large curtains that are hung in strategic locations to "dress" the stage and to prevent the audience from seeing into the **wings** or into the area above the stage. The designations of the curtains can be somewhat confusing because we classify them by different names based on color and fabric, even though they sometimes do the same job.

All the curtains are collectively known by several different names. Perhaps the most proper is the term **soft goods,** which is used to specify all types of fabrics in the official documents that are written to outfit new theatres. It is often shortened to *the goods* or simply *goods* by those who work or perform on the stage. The term *curtain* is widely used and accepted, as is the term *rags,* regardless of the condition of the drapery.

The front curtain is often known as the **main curtain,** the *main rag,* or simply *the main.* The flat curtain at the rear of the stage that is generally lit in a way to represent the sky may be referred to as a **cyc** (short for *cyclorama*), a **sky drop,** or just the **sky.** Curtains that open at the center and travel offstage are known as **bi-parting** and also as **travelers** because the method for opening them is to use a traveler track, where the curtain hangs from rollers that move inside a track. Any curtain that moves on a track can be called a traveler.

The drapery that hangs at the sides of the stage or overhead is collectively known as **masking** because it is used to mask the audience view of the backstage areas. The tall, narrow curtains at the sides of the stage are called **legs** and are typically hung in mirrored pairs on either side of the stage. The wide, short curtains that hang over the width of the stage and mask the view of overhead equipment are called **borders**. This is where it gets a little tricky. The legs that hang at the front of the stage, are made of the same material as the front curtain, and match it in color are called **tormentors**. The border that hangs at the front of the stage, is made of the same material as the front curtain, and matches it in color is called the **teaser**. It can sometimes be called a **valance** too, depending on exactly where it is hung relative to the proscenium and the front curtain.

"In" Positions

All this gets us to the point where we can identify those additional stage locations known as the "in" positions. These terms are generally used to identify where a performer should make an entrance and are particularly useful for dance, where there is typically little or no scenery to identify stage location. An "in one" entrance would take place between the downstage-most leg and the proscenium. "In two" is between the first and second leg, and so on (see figure 3.4). On some stages the "in one" occurs between the tormentor and the proscenium, which changes the relative locations

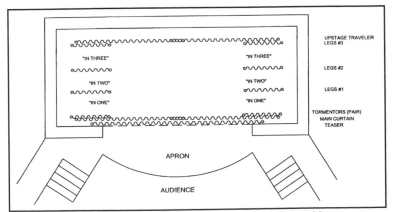

Figure 3.4. Stage floor plan showing drapery and "in" positions

31

of the other entrances, but this is a rare case. As mentioned earlier, these directions can also be used to answer the question "Where does this scene take place?" in staging a musical. "Oh, that's in two" could be the reply. Or one could ask, "Where is that line of dancers for this part?" "They're in one," might be the response from the choreographer.

Now that we have identified the places on the stage where the actors are and where we would aim or focus the lights, we can move on to describing the locations where the lights are placed or "hung."

Identifying Lighting Positions

Stage lighting fixtures are moved often and are typically attached to stage *battens* and other permanent and temporary pipes placed throughout the theatre by means of a **C-clamp**. C-clamps are designed to be attached and removed quickly and to be very secure when properly attached to the correct size pipe. The standard C-clamp in the U.S. is designed to fit on 1 1/2" I.D. Schedule 40 pipe, which is the standard size for stage battens.

We need to be so specific about naming each hanging position in order to be able to communicate where to place each light or direct someone to an instrument for adjustment or service. Horizontal pipes that are used to hang lighting instruments are called **electrics.** They usually have dedicated circuits associated with them, but any batten over the stage or the audience can be deemed an electric if it is used to hang lights. Electrics are numbered sequentially out from the proscenium. So, the first lighting position over the stage is called the "first onstage electric" or the "first electric" and the first position over the audience is called the "first house electric." The next batten over the stage toward the back wall that is designated for lighting is the "second electric" and so on. Following this logic, the next position over the audience toward the rear of the house is the "second house electric" (see figure 3.5).

Single vertical pipes used for lighting are called **booms** and double vertical pipes with rungs between them are known as **light ladders** or simply **ladders.** Booms on the stage are further designated "(stage) left" and "(stage) right" with "number one" indicating the most downstage position (see figure 3.5). Booms in the house are sometimes called **box booms** because they are often placed in areas once occupied by box seats. In some theatres, booms can also be found at the front edge of the balcony on either sidewall and can be referred to as box or balcony booms.

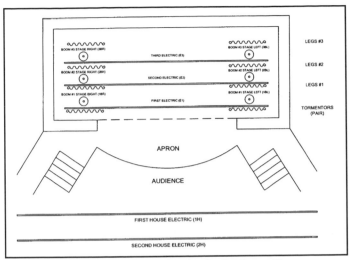

Figure 3.5. Auditorium plan showing lighting positions

A horizontal position at the front of the balcony is the *balcony rail*. Instruments hung in this location typically have a very low **angle of incidence** to the stage and are best used for **curtain warmers** or, in the case of a musical, the conductor **special**. "The rail" can also be used for low-angle blue washes to create realistic nighttime scenes where a flat look and low visual acuity are desirable.

Fixture Names Based on Function

Lighting instruments take on generic names based on where they are located or what function they perform. These labels often cross the lines of fixture type and may be specific to a particular style of production. Keep in mind that, whether you are using a $6,000 robotic fixture or a $6.00 "R" type lamp in a socket, the *function* of the lighting fixture is determined by its *position relative to the object it is lighting.*

Basic Lighting Positions

Any instrument that lights an object from the front can be called a **front light**. These lights are typically located on the house electrics or on the house booms or ladders, but they can also occupy positions on the stage electrics. Lights that are hung directly over the performers are called **down** or **top light**. Light that comes from behind an object and is used to separate it from the background is **backlight**. A top or high backlight is often called a **hair light** in the

33

television industry. Footlights are located on the floor at the front of the stage and are rarely used except for effect. With the exception of footlights, we generally think of fixtures hung in these generic positions as being hung fairly high above the subject they are lighting, with an angle of incidence of 30° or more. Angle of incidence can be briefly described as how far from horizontal a light is, relative to the stage or the subject it is lighting. This is a critical design element and will be examined in detail in later chapters.

Sidelights

Side lighting is light that strikes an object from the side. Sidelights are a prominent part of the stage layout for dance — from ballet to modern and interpretive dance — but they can be used effectively for other types of productions as well. The use of strong side light originated with the ballet and is the accepted convention for dance performances because it brings out detail and accentuates the parts of the body through which the dancers express themselves. Sidelights for dance are typically mounted on booms that are placed in between the masking legs on both sides of the stage. This usually equates to a minimum of six booms, three on each side, even on small stages. Ellipsoidals are most often used for side light and each boom usually carries a minimum of three instruments, and often many more, depending on the level of performance and budget.

Side lighting is divided into three general classifications: "low"(or "lo") to light the feet and legs, "mid" to light the torso, and "high"(or "hi") to light the arms when extended above the body and for lifts. Subclassifications are used when additional equipment is required. The lowest instruments are called **shin busters** (or **shins**) because the instrument is mounted with its center at about one foot off the floor and the unwary dancer may incur a shin injury when exiting into the wings. Instruments that fall into the "mid" category are typically mounted with their centers at two to three feet off the floor, or **deck**, and the "highs" can be five to eight feet or more off the floor. It is important to avoid placing instruments at about six to seven feet off the floor, where they will blind the dancers when they are onstage and may cause injuries to the face and head should a mishap occur as the dancers exit past the booms into the wings.

Another type of side lighting that is used frequently in traditional productions as well as dance is **high side light.** These instruments may start at the offstage ends of the battens or on pipe-mounted ladders and can continue onstage past the centerline. If they are located only at the offstage ends of the pipes, they are called **pipe ends.**

Strip Lights, Specials, and Uplights

Strip lights, or fixtures with three or more large "cells" called *cyc lights* or *far cycs* that carry an intense source in each cell, can all fall into the category of **cyc lighting.** A **special** can be any type of fixture that has a singular purpose. It may be used to light a specific area and be identified as "bench special" or to light a certain performer for a particular moment and be called, for instance, the "Maria special." In any case, a special is an instrument that is added to the overall plot for the express purpose of creating a moment or a particular look that is distinct from the way the rest of the show looks.

One last term that identifies instruments by their function and position is **uplight.** As the name implies, uplight is used in those unusual cases where a subject is lit from below. Keep in mind that the fixture designations that describe function cross the lines of specific fixture types and are an integral part of design language.

Chapter Four
Light: The Designer's Paint

The Specular Quality of Light

Now that we have examined the different fixtures that create the light — the "paint brushes" if you will — and their placement, we can begin to study the medium that they emit — the light, or "paint" in the artist analogy.

As mentioned earlier, the quality of the light that is produced by different fixtures varies and has an affect on the way we perceive the lighted object. Some of the information that our brain uses to qualify the nature of light is contained in the shadows that are created by the light. Additional information is provided by how the light is reflected off the objects that it strikes.

In general, we consider the light that is emitted by fixtures that produce a distinct beam or hard edge as being more specular in nature. This characterization typically applies to fixtures in the ellipsoidal family, but it could also describe the light produced by a Fresnel with the lens removed. In the latter example, the perceived specular quality is produced by the light bouncing off the highly polished reflector as well as the raw light from the lamp itself. Conversely, fixtures that emit a soft pool of light or cover a broad area, such as Fresnels, scoops, and strip lights, are considered to be less specular in nature. They produce soft shadows and seamless modeling.

The differences in specular quality among lights is subtle and probably does not register consciously for most audience members, but it does figure into the overall look and perception of the show. We often combine fixtures of varying specular characteristics in a **Light Plot,** and it is important for the designer to be aware of the differences. Variations in specular quality can have an unconscious effect on how the audience perceives a shift in the lighting as a performer transitions from an area of being lit primarily by one type of fixture to an area lit by fixtures with a different specular characteristic.

Specular quality can be modified through the use of diffusion media or, in the case of robotic fixtures, by variable lens arrangements, but for the fixtures we have discussed so far the specular qualities of a particular fixture remain constant.

Lighting the Actor's Face

The essence of lighting design is to affect what the audience sees through careful control of the "paint" (light) coming from the "brush" (fixture). You will note that much of the discussion regarding how the light looks will reference the performer's face. This is because we look at faces for a wealth of information on many levels in our day-to-day interactions with others. This is a natural practice that carries over into theatregoing.

Simply put, the face of the performer is the most important object we light. Nothing else has the power to convey emotion and support the meaning of the work in the way the performer's face does. The most eloquent piece of spoken text can be lost through poor lighting because there is a psychological connection between seeing the face and understanding speech. The connection is so strong that the audience is convinced that, if they can't see, they can't hear either. This is not to say that we can ignore or treat lightly the requirement to light every aspect of the production, but lighting the face is extremely important.

This is true even in dance, where we concentrate most of the lighting equipment, and expend a great deal of effort, on lighting the body. The ability to see facial expression completes the picture for the audience, and it is vital to the success of any performance. As mentioned earlier, dance productions are lit mainly with side light from booms in the wings, but if we are unable to properly light the dancers' faces from the sides or introduce a bit of front light to help the audience see the faces, we create an annoying sensation that can't be ignored by the audience. As a result, the audience will respond poorly to each piece in which we neglect to light faces adequately.

The Controllable Qualities of Light

Control of light, and how light is perceived when it is reflected from any object, is the basis of the artistic element of design. The following section of our exploration addresses what are known as the four controllable qualities of light in stage design: angle, intensity, movement, and color.

Angle

McCandless Style

When we refer to lighting angles, we are talking about angle in two different planes or categories. One category identifies the angle by *function* (front, top, side, or back) and the other refers to the *angle of incidence* of the light to the subject. In both cases we are making a three-dimensional consideration of angle, always relative to the object that is being lit. An introduction to this concept and the craft of lighting the stage would not be complete without a discussion of the McCandless theory of lighting the stage.

Early in the twentieth century, Stanley McCandless (1900–1967) developed a method for lighting the acting areas of the stage that has been a starting point for nearly all designers who have followed. Simply put, the McCandless "method" states that the best way to light a performer from the front is with two fixtures at a 45° angle from either side, left and right of the performer, with both at a 45° angle of incidence, or down angle, from above. (For a graphic representation of this concept see figures 4.1 and 4.2.)

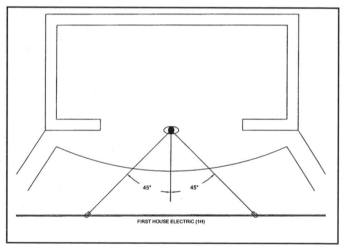

Figure 4.1. Plan view of McCandless lighting

The basis for using two fixtures at the prescribed angles lies in the fact that we are used to seeing a mixture of primary and reflected light that creates natural modeling on the face. This phenomenon is not apparent to most people, but the concept is crucial to designers. If you think about it, the logic carries the theory through. On a sunny day, there is a strong primary source, the sun, on one side of the face and light that has been reflected from trees, grass, buildings, windows, etc., on the other. Some objects reflect light differently than others and some impart coloration to the reflected light. The apparent color of sunlight is modified by the atmosphere as the Earth rotates through its daily cycle. All these considerations affect our choice of color media from each direction for a given set of conditions that we are to create.

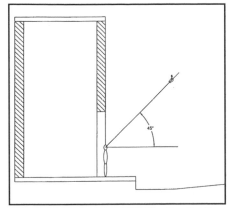

Figure 4.2. Section view of McCandless lighting

It is often not possible to hang instruments in a precise McCandless configuration due to constraints imposed by the building. The angle of incidence is fixed by the position of the lighting gallery (catwalk) where the lights are hung. In well planned theatres, we can usually count on a Front-of-House lighting position where the lights hang at right around 45° angles relative to the downstage areas. Typically, however, the theatre is not wide enough to allow a 45° angle to the areas that are closer to the extreme stage left and right portions of the stage and the apron. Narrowing the angle to around 30–35° will generally resolve the issue. We have to keep in mind, though, that we need to keep the angle as consistent as possible throughout the plot.

We will cover this in more detail later, but as we start to develop our lighting craft, we need to keep in mind that the McCandless method has been successful because it compliments the face with natural modeling and color and provides good visual acuity for the audience. When we depart from this practice, we have to understand the impetus for the departure and how it will affect audience perception. Following are some examples of those departures and why they are important design tools.

Non-McCandless Lighting Styles
Straight in Wash

One of the most frequently used deviations from the 45° method that falls into the category of front light is the **straight in wash.** This consists of a series of fixtures that are hung on axis with (directly in front of) the subject to be lit. In other words, the fixture is *not* hung 30–45° to the side of the acting area but is focused

39

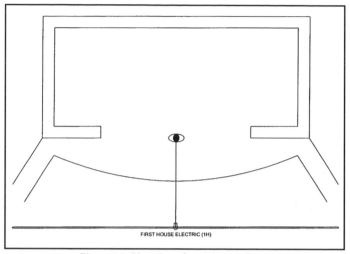

Figure 4.3. Plan view of straight in lighting

perpendicular to the proscenium to light the subject (see figure 4.3). Because the **yoke** of the fixture is not rotated on the axis of the C-clamp, the focus is said to be straight in.

The resulting lack of modeling, which tends to make objects look flat, is particularly useful when colored blue and used for night scenes. It is surprising how much light can exist on the stage, in terms of foot-candles, while still making it very clear to the audience that a nighttime scene is being played on the stage. Blue light is typically associated with night, but it is the *angle* of the light that reduces modeling and creates the "flatness" that makes the audience think it is dark and difficult to see. A straight-in angle can create a most convincing nighttime scene while giving the performers plenty of light to work in. Especially when combined with the low angle of incidence of a balcony rail, it is usually necessary to supplement the "night wash" with some additional light that produces modeling in order to avoid complaints from the audience that they can't see.

Side Lighting

As mentioned earlier, another common departure from the McCandless method is the way that ballet and dance are lit. Strong, specular light, usually from ellipsoidals, pours onto the stage from the wings from floor level to the ends of the overhead battens. This convention allows the designer to selectively create extreme modeling on the dancers' forms, using intense colors without making the face look grotesque. That key element of the face,

40

although not the primary focus, must look natural for the performance to be a success. (That is, of course, unless a particular piece is *supposed* to create a feeling of mystery or perhaps represent dark spirits.) Some splashes of intense color on the face from the sidelight are acceptable for dance performances, but most designers will tend toward more moderate color selections for the fixtures on the booms that are near head height.

Alternative Angles

The classic "bad" angle is the "monster" light from the flashlight held under the face. Footlights were introduced as a matter of practicality, and their use was abandoned as soon as an alternative became available because of the unnatural look they gave to the face as well as the tall shadows they cast on any scenery behind the actors. This is a most unnatural angle, but it can be put to good use when it is not concentrated on the face and used as uplight. Today, many touring stages are built with thick Plexiglas flooring to take advantage of this useful and dramatic option. Especially when used in conjunction with particulate matter in the air (smoke, fog, or haze) uplight can create an uplifting sense of ascension.

There are many other instances where balanced 45° angles may not be the best approach. Natural situations such as sunsets, moonlight, and rainy days give us opportunities to experiment with alternative angles. Fantastic stories told in words, music, and dance offer even greater freedom to enhance the audience experience and broaden your use of angle to produce a different lighting environment.

Intensity

Intensity is the component of design on which we spend the most time within the collective context of rehearsal. Writing cues and adjusting intensity levels is a major component of the tech week process and it involves the entire production team. (Writing cues and the other more collaborative aspects of lighting design are addressed in the last part of this book.)

Intensity as we perceive it in the theatre can be defined as the apparent brightness of an object *relative to the objects around it*. The relative nature of intensity is an important factor in a successful design and it begins with the house light cues at the top of the show. We manipulate the house lights in particular ways to indicate to the audience how they should behave at a particular moment and to focus their attention. Dimming the house lights to begin a production not only indicates to the audience that the show is about

41

to begin and it's time to settle into their seats, but it also brings to a peak the brightness adaptation that began when they first entered the theatre.

BRIGHTNESS ADAPTATION

Brightness adaptation is the phenomenon that takes place when we move from a place of relative brightness to an area of relative darkness. Described in mechanical terms, it is the time it takes the iris in the eye to expand in order to allow more light into the retina, or, conversely, the time it takes the iris to contract to let in less light. It is why we cover our eyes when we are subjected to bright light after being in a dark place, like a theatre. We squint and cover our eyes because they have not had time to respond to the increased brightness and reduce the amount of light that is allowed to enter.

Brightness adaptation is an important factor to keep in mind when writing cues and rehearsing during the day. If you're in the middle of a sequence and take a break to go outside, your frame of reference when you come in and get right back to work has changed considerably. Many cues have been rewritten or adjusted because the brightness adaptation that the audience experiences was not duplicated during the rehearsal process. This is not to say that you should remain in a darkened theatre for the entire cuing procedure, just be aware that your eye is always at work adjusting light levels and that you need to give yourself a little time to adjust. With practice, you can begin to train your brain to compensate to some degree, but you will want to check those cuing sequences when your brightness adaptation matches what the audience experience will be. Brightness adaptation is only one of the ways in which the eye functions in its quest to satisfy the brains' desire for visual input.

THE HUMAN RESPONSE TO INTENSITY

The way that the eye responds to light and color is quite remarkable, and that, along with the way that the brain interprets the signals that come from the eyes, are factors to be considered in the development of a cohesive lighting design that supports the work being presented. The process of brightness adaptation is the means to an end, that end being focusing the attention of the audience to the place where we want it, and *only* there, typically the stage. Our eyes and our brain work in conjunction with each other to always regard the area that has the highest apparent brightness as that which is most important, and we will automatically look there. Our brain may modify that axiom if it regards some action as being vital to survival, such as forcing us to squint when we look into the sun while driving a car or try to identify a person who is standing in front of a blinding light source. But, for the most part, good stage design is rooted in skillfully steering the attention of the audience around the stage by manipulating intensity and color so that everyone will naturally look where we intended them to.

The antithesis of a purposely brightly lit area that draws the attention of the audience to a place where we want it is a dark spot that calls attention to itself where we don't want it. Everyone notices a dark spot or dip in the lighting because our eyes and brain are looking for evenness in the lighted environment. While we will ignore moderate shadowing on the face when we are outdoors, we are very unforgiving of even slight variations in intensity on a performer as they walk across the stage. This is partly because we *know* the stage is being lit artificially and that designers should not allow such poor shadowing to creep into the lighted environment they create, but it is also because we are focusing intently on the words being spoken and an unjustified change in the way the lighting looks is distracting. The exception, of course, is when patterns are used to cast a specific shadow or "break up" the light. Audiences understand this convention and accept it as long as there is enough balanced light on the performers to see their facial expression.

Finally, a review of the Robert Edmond Jones' statement that "lighting design is putting light where you want it and taking it away where you don't" reminds us that focus cannot only be achieved by increasing the intensity on a certain spot, but also by *reducing* intensity in surrounding areas. In the technical sense, intensity is merely how bright or dim the setting on the control is for a particular instrument. In later sections, we will see how the series of numbers that represent different intensities and make up the cues for a show can work together to create a truly artistic and moving expression.

Movement

THE NATURE OF LIGHTING CHANGES

When we use the word *movement* with regard to lighting in the modern world, it is a term that can be easily confused. One might think that movement applies only to the current proliferation of robotic fixtures that are gaining more acceptance and popularity. In fact, the term has been used to describe an aspect of lighting that existed long before robotic fixtures were even dreamed of. Actually, the term has to do with the topic we just visited, intensity. Intensity, however, is simply a level set on a control console or the brightness of a light. At times, some members of the production team do use the two terms interchangeably in that they may say that, for a given lighting change, they didn't see a particular fixture "move." This is simply a diplomatic way of saying that they didn't see a change in intensity. Movement, in the context that we are currently examining, refers to the changes in light levels *in real time*. In other words, it acknowledges not only a shift in the lighted environment of the stage picture, but also how long it took for the lights that were increasing in intensity to come up, how long it took for the lights that were decreasing in intensity to go down, and how long the overall change took.

THE ARTISTRY OF MOVEMENT

When we analyze movement in this way, it seems somewhat dry and unimaginative, but movement in stage lighting is one of the areas where the *art* of lighting is most apparent and the designer can be most expressive in supporting the production. Because movement is such a powerful tool, it is also one of the areas where mistakes and errors in judgment can be detrimental to a production, particularly when we recognize that the lighting changes have a rhythm and they set the pace for the show. If the rhythm of the movement matches the mood and tempo of the moment, it supports the production; if it doesn't, it makes the production seem awkward and choppy. This applies not only to the cues that begin and end scenes, but to all the "internal" cueing as well.

Let's explore the mechanics of movement to see how they affect the impression of the production. We need to keep in mind that we are not looking at hard and fast rules, but only examples of what could be appropriate in a general sense. Decisions regarding cue speed and timing are specific to each production. There would nearly always be some justification to take the opposite approach to any of the following scenarios.

It's not hard to imagine that a crisp **blackout** at the end of a scene where the hero has just died and the ingénue is singing him a tearful goodbye might not be appropriate. Conversely, if the light on the lovers lingers too long after the song has ended, the audience will start squirming in their seats because they are uncomfortable. There is a fine line as to how long they can be emotionally connected to the tragedy. Similarly, using a **bump** cue to bring the lights up for the first time on the home of the sisters in *Arsenic and Old Lace* would probably seem jarring to most audience members.

Emphasizing the entrance of a major character with a lighting change that doesn't fit that character's personality or that is not in keeping with the moment is likely to provoke laughter rather than the empathy that was intended. The laughter signifies that the audience is, again, uncomfortable, and not that they recognize something "wrong" with the movement of the light. Movement is a powerful tool in lighting and the style and timing of each change; whether it's a quick blackout or a long sunset cue, the movement must fit the moment in order to support the production.

Color is another powerful element of lighting and, as we will see in the next section, can be used to make things clear to the audience or to confuse and confound them.

Color

Color is often considered to be one of the most difficult aspects of lighting design to master. Selection of color may seem intimidating for two reasons. One, because there are simply so many colors manufactured in the form of Mylar film to choose from, and two, the use of color is regarded as being closely associated with the emotion and psychology of the production. The psychology of color is a topic that is foreign to most of us as we begin to light shows.

The phrase "experience is the best teacher" rings true for developing lighting skills in general, and it seems particularly applicable to selection and use of color. This is not to say that young designers can't come up with good designs — quite the opposite is true — but each time we light a production, see someone else's work, or experience a different natural lighting phenomenon, we have more information in our mental "lighting library" to choose from.

The *only* rule that applies universally to color selection is to be willing to try *anything*, at least in the light lab or in rehearsal. Completely changing the color in a show the night before opening is probably not done without risk, but we all have this experience, and some more than once. There are some things that we know about the mechanism of the eye that can help us down the path to successful color selection, but first we need to explore how the color is created and how colors in lighting interact with each other.

THE PRIMARIES AND MIXING

Obviously, all of our experiences related to physical sight depend on light being reflected off *something*, and the color characteristics of the light source and the object off which the light is reflected affect what we "see." *See* is in quotes here because the visual information that enters as light through our eyes travels a path through the experiential filters in our brains, and what we *think* we see is not always what is actually there. The (color of) light affects how we see the colors of the painting, and the color of the surface that the light strikes affects our perception of the color of the light. Keep in mind that we cannot perceive light unless it is being reflected off an object, whether it be an actor, a set piece, or a smoke particle.

There are two initial concepts relating to color in lighting that are different than our past experience with other media. First, the primary colors of light are red, blue, and green, as opposed to red, blue, and yellow in other media, such as paint. Second, (and the reason that the primary colors are different) is that the color mixing that takes place in lighting is *additive* rather than subtractive as it is with other types of media. This concept is supported by the fact that, when we mix the primary colors of light together, we get *white* light, instead of the dark brown muddy color that we got when we mixed the primaries in junior paint sets together in our elementary school days. If we look at it from the other direction, we say that black paint contains all the colors of paint mixed together, but it is white light that contains all the colors of light.

The latter concept can be demonstrated by using a prism to separate white light into the component parts of the spectrum. It's difficult to separate a blob of black paint into its component parts, but we understand what's going on there from experience. The reason that color mixing in lighting is called additive is that when different colors of light are reflected off a neutral surface, the colors combine to bring the resultant closer to white light, not closer to a mix of muddy brown. When we look at a painting, the colors we perceive in the pigment are those colors of light that are reflected and *not* absorbed. Color mixing in painting is called subtractive because, as we add pigments together, less and less of the full spectrum of visible light is reflected as more is absorbed. Conversely, as we mix more and more colors of light together, the resulting combination that is reflected off an object is closer to the full spectrum of white.

COLOR MEDIA

The colors of paint are created by adding pigment to a base or "vehicle" that will carry the pigment, adhere to a surface, and dry to the desired finish. Color in lighting is created by placing a filter in front of the source that absorbs certain frequencies or colors of white light and transmits only colors in the desired range. Originally, tinted glass was used for this purpose because the technology for creating colored glass had been in existence for quite some time. Also, colored glass presented no fire hazard when used with sources that were based on combustion and produced considerable amounts of heat. We typically use tinted glass in the form of roundels to produce consistent primary colors in strip lights today.

The filters that we use for other types of instruments are manufactured from sheets of plastic that are formulated with the color as part of the media. Each filter color is given a number according to a scheme determined by the manufacturer. Along with assigning a number to each color, manufacturers choose a name for each color they create. This practice began when lighting filters were made from a gelatin base and the available selection of colors was fairly limited. The archaic term **gel,** a holdover from this period, is still prevalent, along with the naming of each new color that is introduced.

Although names such as "no color blue," "straw," and "special lavender" are common to most of the lines manufactured today, the transmissivity (the colors that are transmitted through the filter) and the resulting color of the filtered light are not the same across manufacturers. If your distributor is unable to provide a color from a certain manufacturer in time for a production, direct number substitution of a color from another manufacturer is not always the best answer. You may be forced to consider changing the entire color palette of the show in order to achieve the correct color balance for the production. Although this can be a considerable setback when time is at a premium, the result can be better overall than the original palette would have rendered.

Now that we have looked at how the colors of light mix together and understand the mechanics of color mixing with light, we can begin to explore how audiences perceive color and the ways color can be used in the theatre.

THE MEANING OF COLOR

Our perceptions of color and the association to what certain colors "mean" to us are based not only on our experience in the natural world but also in the collective whole of our visual encounters. This includes painting, photography, film, video, and theatre, as well as all other forms of art and natural occurrences. As our library of visual reference grows throughout our lifetime, we categorize certain visual characteristics with a certain time of day, a specific type of event, or a particular emotion. This is known associative learning, where we associate one thing, in this case color, with a certain perception or feeling based on our past experience. Some of these associations are more universal than others and we can site them as impressions that hold true for most of the general population.

Again, the discussion that follows is not a set of rules but merely generally accepted conventions and some factual information about how the eye works. Remember, the only rule in working with color in lighting is to try *everything*. Continue to experiment with different combinations of color throughout the time that the subject is of interest to you. All too often, we fall into a pattern of using colors in a certain range for lighting from particular angles because we can visualize the result from our experience and we are comfortable that we won't be embarrassed by the result when we begin to cue the show. This creates a luminous environment that allows the audience to see well, but the light is generic and doesn't go to the heart of truly supporting the production by being specifically appropriate to each moment. Keep in mind during your experiments that lighting does not typically exist only unto itself, but is used to provide illumination and to support the overall production initiatives.

Cool Colors: Blue = Night

One of the fairly universally accepted generalities regarding the color of light is that blue light indicates a nighttime scene. This stems from our experience in the natural world, but also from years of conditioning through film, television, and theatre. It doesn't seem to matter which direction the blue light comes from. It can come from the front, side, back, top, or the sky as long as it is more saturated than the blue we are using for daytime scenes. The notion that blue equals night is well established in most audience members, so we have to be aware that the "nighttime" message is fairly easily sent. The range of blue that telegraphs the night trigger to most people falls into a fairly saturated portion of the blue range, so there are plenty of blues that we can use for scenes that take place at other times without fear of saying "night" to the audience.

Warm Colors: Red = Intense Emotion

Red is another color that has a fairly strong associative context, but the range is a bit broader than that of blue. The various shades of red are typically associated with heat, danger, passion, or the occult. The association with heat comes from our natural experience with fire, and the connection with the occult stems from our historical notions of intense heat in the underworld. The association of red with danger and passion comes through the emotion that is common to both, which is fear. When we feel threatened by a dangerous situation, our instinct for survival kicks in so that we can rescue ourselves and be relieved of the fear. Passion, in the broad sense, can be thought of as either intense love or intense anger. In either case, fear is the motivator, either fear of losing something precious to us, fear of being vulnerable, or fear that we may be overcome by an idea or belief system with which we do not agree.

The fact that red is one of the primary colors of light, coupled with the way our eye reacts to red light and our learned response to red, all add up to the general perception that there is *intense emotion* associated with any activity that takes place in red light. The more surprising aspect of our reaction to red light is that it covers such a broad range of emotional states.

The Lavender Range

It is also interesting to note at this point that the eye cannot perceive red light and blue light in the same place at the same time. This is not to say that we couldn't see a pool of red light next to a pool of blue light, but the fact that the interaction between the rods and cones in the eye does not allow us to see them in the same instant can be a useful tool for the lighting designer.

The colors that literally "blur the lines" between being warm and cool are those that fall into the lavender range. The reason for this becomes obvious when we examine the wavelength transmission chart that accompanies each swatch of color and identifies it by name and number (see figure 4.4). You will notice that most of the lavenders have high transmission rates in both the blue and red wavelengths. This characteristic is useful in two ways. First, if you need to light a scene in such a way that the level of detail that the audience can perceive is low, a lavender will do the trick. This is because the red and blue components are fairly well balanced and the eye has difficulty focusing. Some older performers are only lit in lavender light for this very reason. When used on aging performers, the combination of some of the lavenders with colors in the pink range is very complimentary and pleasing.

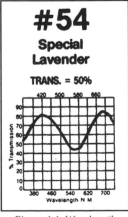

Figure 4.4. Wavelength transmission chart

The second, and perhaps more useful, application of the characteristics of lavender light is that colors in this family can be used as the warm *or* cool complement, depending on the other color with which they are mixed. In conjunction with this, the lavenders change character depending on the intensity of the light. Some of the lavenders will be perceived as cool when the channel is at or near full but look much warmer when the light is "run down on dimmer," because the lamp filament outputs much more light in the red frequency range as the intensity is reduced. This can be a particularly useful feature when you are working with a limited fixture inventory. There is great utility in all these features, but try not to become so enchanted by them that you use lavender for every show.

You may also be surprised to note that some of the colors in the blue family are formulated in such a way that the wavelength curves have some fairly evenly distributed peaks in the red and blue ranges. This information can be particularly helpful when you are choosing a blue for an application where it will be operated at very low intensities.

Color Reversal and Negative After-imaging

Two devices that we can use with an audience that are a natural outcome of our experiments with primary colors and with light are those of **color reversal** and **negative after-imaging.** The degree of usefulness that these phenomena have is somewhat limited with an audience, due to the inevitable restlessness that will result if an audience is left in the dark too long. But knowing how our eyes and brain work together to create a certain perception is valuable as we develop our talents in lighting. Some experimentation along these lines is useful. Please keep in mind that our initial adventures with these trials should be conducted in a controlled environment where everyone is aware of the objective.

You will notice that if you stare at red light focused on a white surface in a darkened room for about thirty to sixty seconds or so and then turn off the red light source and close your eyes, you will see a *green* afterimage where the red light was. This is also true when you lie on the beach with your eyes closed facing up at the sun without sunglasses on. In this case, the white sunlight is filtered through the tiny blood vessels in your eyelids, which is why you perceive the color red when your eyes are closed under brightly lit conditions. When you open your eyes and look around, your visual field is filtered through the reversed green afterimage until your eyes have had a chance to adapt to the new condition. The opposite is true when green light is used as the source. Try experiments with blue and with pools of primary light colors focused on a white or lightly colored surface. Your eye and brain will always produce an exact complement to the color being viewed.

Negative after-imaging is the term that is used to describe the condition that occurs when a white light source is removed after the eye has been exposed to a lighted scene for a period of time. In this case, when the light is turned off and we are left in darkness, those objects that were brightly lit reverse to dark images surrounded by a brighter field. Areas that were in shadow when the light was on are translated into being the brightest parts of the reversed image.

The practice of isolating a single performer in an intense light is sometimes referred to as "burning" an image into the eyes of the audience. This is not to say that we should attempt to inflict damage on the collective vision of the audience, but we can use our knowledge of certain devices and how the eye operates to telegraph powerful messages to the audience. The lingering image may not be highly detailed, but it can be perceived fairly quickly and will be present in the subconscious regardless of what follows. This phenomenon has greater utility than the color reversal scenario in an audience situation, but experimentation with the various effects of color and image reversal under controlled conditions is strongly encouraged.

COLOR SELECTION AND PRODUCTION STYLE

Color saturation, or how vivid the colors are, is a factor that is, to some degree, determined by the type of production that is being lit. Straight ("regular") plays that take place in a natural environment are typically lit with a less saturated range of colors, except at those times when we are called upon to create a more dramatic naturalistic look, such as a sunset. Again, this standard is based on the style of each production, and the use of more vibrant colors can certainly be used to enhance the visual context of a play. This twist on the purely natural is particularly useful in some of the classics that are well known on the basis of their literary merits but can use a boost in their production value for today's audiences.

Musicals generally take more liberties in their visual appearance, particularly lighting, as they are a departure from the naturalistic norm. The next step up the scale is operas, which are generally considered to have a heightened sense of reality. Here, the general tone of the lighting can take flight to enhance the opulent scenic and costuming elements common to this production style. The use of more saturated, less naturalistic colors is based on the caveat that the featured singers in a particular segment will be lit with follow spots within the context of the rest of the luminous environment. For dance creations we not only change the angle of the primary lighting to the side, but we can also make bold color selections based on the theme of each piece and the costumes that are worn. Finally, we move into the realm of performance art, alternative theatre, and rock 'n' roll. In the case of rock 'n' roll, as in opera, follow spots are heavily relied upon to pick out the featured performers and provide the visual acuity we need to see them while allowing us to appreciate the rich visual atmosphere encompassing them.

The selection of color is a process of discovery, based in the context of a particular production and on the trials, errors, and experience that we gain as we develop our craft into an art. Our efforts to this end should not strive to create a "trademark style" or to stagnate in the tried and true, but always to provide light to the performers that enhances the overall production and increases the fulfillment of its objectives for the audience.

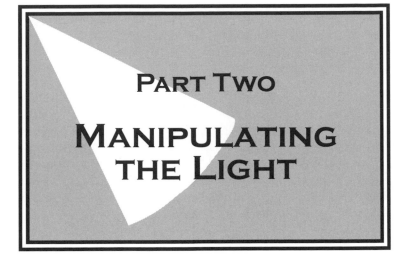

Part Two

Manipulating the Light

Chapter Five
Developing the Lighting Key

In order to manipulate the lighting in harmony with the progression of a production, we must first create a lighting scheme. We do this by understanding the rationale behind the lighting. This task is performed in conjunction with reading and analyzing the script and understanding the **concept** for the production as well as the themes present in the work of the other designers.

An aide to discovering and documenting the basis for the lighting is called the **Lighting Key.** The Lighting Key is a simple diagram that gives us a graphic representation of how we think the light for the show is created, and it gives us a starting point upon which to base our decisions about the lighting for the entire production. As we will see later in this text, the Light Plot is an extension or repetition of the Lighting Key.

The Lighting Key has two major functions. One is to show the type and color of filter media we intend to use in a fixture, but more importantly to *name the source* that we are identifying with that color. Using this method, we can develop a clear understanding of the context for the lighting in any production.

Identifying the Sources

The essential purpose of the Lighting Key is to identify the sources of the light. Often our choices are based in the naturalistic context of a play, but they can diverge into fantastic worlds that have yet to be imagined. For the purposes of this exercise, we will begin with a naturalistic setting on a proscenium stage.

Let's say we are lighting a box set that has some windows in it, with the main entrance in the upstage half of the stage right wall (see figure 5.1). After observing several rehearsals, we notice a pattern in the blocking where the main characters enter through the upstage right door and stand facing downstage left, "cheating" out to the audience to deliver important lines and lengthy speeches. This is where the rehearsal process becomes a key factor in helping to develop the lighting design. If we are to assume that this interior

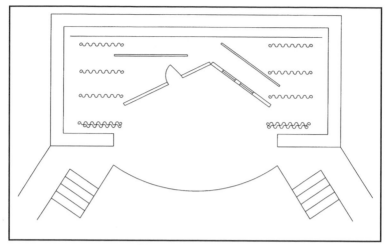

Figure 5.1. Plan of box set

set is to be lit by daylight for some parts of the play, it would be advantageous to imagine the sun coming from house right (stage left) and place it on that side using a McCandless-style plot. In this way, when the actors enter through the main door, they are welcomed to the stage by the warm light of the "sun" angled squarely on their faces.

This can be an easy way to make the decision regarding "on which side do I put the warm and where do I put the cool" in the front light. We do need to look at the production as a whole and consider how the cool light from house left will play in each scene, but the basis of this major decision about the front lighting can be made in this way. The result is lighting that complements the production and is not in conflict with the blocking. Take a moment to consider how the audience would receive the actor's lines differently if the warm and cool colors were reversed in the plot.

Assigning Color to the Sources
Front Light

In our sample, we have identified the sun as coming from house right and, after looking through the swatch book provided by the manufacturer, have decided to use R (Roscolux) 08 to represent the color of the sun in this particular production. Keep in mind that lighting designers and stage electricians will always refer to color by identifying the manufacturer and color number. To the uninitiated, a conversation about color using only letters and numbers seems very odd, but with all the different shades of color and an increasing variety of manufacturers, it is the only way to correctly identify a particular color filter. Occasionally, the designer or electrician will refer to the "red wash" or, perhaps, the "blue backlight" or "lavender special," but only when speaking in general terms about something that can be readily acknowledged. These terms could be used interchangeably with the "L 182 wash" the "G 815 backlight" or the "R 54 special" if a more precise method of identification is required. When developing the Lighting Key, however, the emphasis on naming the source takes priority over choosing the precise color that will represent that source. The selection of color will come as a natural extension of identifying what the sources are, coupled with other information from the text, the overall mood of the piece, and the other visual elements of the production, such as scenery and costumes.

In our current example, we have classified the source as the sun and assigned a color to it, but what is the source of and the justification for the front light that comes from the other side of this McCandless-style light plot? If you recall, in our earlier exploration of natural daylight, we found that we perceive the sun as the primary source, but we also perceive a secondary source in the reflected light. The reflected light is the color we perceive on the unlit side of the face, which is the color that is present in the sky. On a sunny day this is typically a shade of blue, or at least a color in the cool family. This notion of sunlight on one side of the face and the predominance of blue on the other is the basis for the practice of using a "warm side" and "cool side" color scheme for the front light for many productions. This is not to say that we must always balance the use of a color in the straw, pink, or amber family with a blue, lavender, or green, but it is a convention that can serve as a starting point for nearly every style of lighting. For the interior scene in our current exercise, we must consider the reflected light from the walls, but it is the blue of the sky coming through the windows that is considered to be the predominant secondary source. Remember that you must use two light sources focused to the same area in order to observe the results of true additive color mixing. Holding two color swatches in front of a single light source blocks additional frequencies of light and the resulting blend of color is a *subtractive* mix of the two swatches.

For this naturalistic play, we will want to choose a cool complement to the sun color that falls in a similar range of **value** as the color we have chosen for the sun. In other words, we will want to use a color that has about the same saturation level of blue as the saturation level of warm tones in the sun color. Therefore, after referring to the swatch book again, we might start off with a choice of R 62 for our cool side color and see if it will carry through the production as a viable selection. This is not an indication of a preference for a particular brand of color media, but serves to simplify the study of our sample Key by keeping the references to color limited to one swatch book. Mixing of different brands of color in a production is certainly allowed, and encouraged, if it is required to achieve equilibrium in the color palette that you have chosen. It complicates the color order to some degree, but having the correct colors serves to maintain the integrity of the design.

Top and Backlight

Now that we have made our preliminary choices for the warm and cool front colors, we arrive at the point where we need to select the color(s) for the top and/or backlight. In our example we will consider only backlight. Keeping in mind that the function of backlight is to separate the performers from the background, in this case the set, we must also choose a color that works in conjunction with the colors in the front light to support the illusion that this play exists in the world of natural illumination for a particular season, locale, and time of day. We must also remember that all of our choices must also support the action and the emotional context of the production. A common choice for backlight color is a blue that is somewhat more saturated than the cool-side blue of the front light. In our example, something along the lines of R 64 might do nicely.

There are a number of reasons that a slightly richer blue backlight can work well in this scenario. First, it serves to carve the performers out of the surrounding scenery by creating a distinguishing environment between them and the walls of the set. Second, it supports the simulation of reflected light by introducing another layer of color that can be varied in intensity to track the time of day and the emotion of the play. This is to say that we can use the blue backlight to define a scene at night, while using the warm and the cool light from the front to illuminate the performers in a way that mimics lamps in the room, which provides the justification for adequate light levels so the audience can see the action.

We have more latitude with the color selection and the intensity of the backlight because the audience will typically only perceive the effect of the backlight, while not being acutely aware of the light itself. Although we have selected a shade of blue for the backlight in our example, there is nothing to say that a shade of lavender (or some other color) wouldn't be an acceptable or, perhaps, a better choice. It all depends on how literal we choose to be with the lighting in terms of the naturalistic aspects of the production, the other means we use to establish time of day, and what supports the emotional atmosphere that defines the context of the interaction between the players.

Identifying the Elements and Their Relationships

Now that we have established a Lighting Key through the identification of the sources and assigning direction and our preliminary color choices to them, let's examine the elements of the key and their relationships. The first source that we identified was the sun. It is the primary source and the predominant color of light for the production. For this reason it is known as the **key light.** This term comes to us from the world of film and television, but it is applicable in describing the function of this element. The secondary source in our example is the blue front light, which represents the reflected or **fill light,** so named because it fills in the shadows on the side of the face unlit by the key light. Finally, top light or backlight helps to pull the performers out of the background and define the stage picture. The term used for top or backlight in film and television is *hair light,* and its reference is useful in reminding us where to look as we select colors and set intensity levels for this important element of the lighting recipe. The Lighting Key can contain other components as well, such as a low, orange-amber side light to represent a sunset, or a pale blue from a steep front, side, or back angle to represent the moon on a clear night.

Summary of the Lighting Key and Its Applications

In summary, the importance of the Lighting Key is twofold. First, it helps us to define *what* the sources are. Second, it helps us to locate *where* the sources are and where the strongest source is, which doesn't always have to be from a front light position.

Defining the source is not always a literal reference to the time of day. It takes into account such things as the locale, the season, and the weather, but is even more closely tied to the emotional content of the scene and the play as a whole. Identifying the sources is

59

especially important when we light a fantastical production, or a scene that takes place in a fairy tale, on another planet, or in another world. We may be making up the entire context of the lighted environment, but we must imagine what the sources are and how the light is created in order to know what colors and angles to use, where the key light is located, what the reflected light looks like (and why), and how the light plays upon the performers and all of the visual elements of the production.

Once we know what the sources are, whether it be the sun, the moon, reflected light from the sky, or a mysterious light from an as yet unimagined source, then we know where to place the light that represents that source. When we have an idea about what is creating the light and we tie that together with our understanding of the production including the context, emotion, action, and production style, the choice of color grows naturally out of the work instead of being "applied" by the designer.

Chapter Six
Assigning Intensity Levels

Once we have established the Lighting Key, we can begin to think about varying intensities to create visual interest, crafting the play of light and shadow in each scene, and developing a progression of cues in a way that will support the production. Earlier it was noted that the most significant amount of collective and collaborative time that is spent on the lighting design is in writing and adjusting the cues. Cue writing is nothing more than assigning intensity levels from zero to full for each instrument at every moment in the production. But we are willing to invest so much of everyone's time in finalizing the cues because it is vitally important to the success of each moment and, ultimately, the show.

If we think in terms of intensity, we can agree that, in general, the intensity of a naturalistic night scene will be less than that of a typical daytime scene in the same play. Our current discussion of intensity will seek to go beyond such basic observations by exploring the subtleties of creating visual interest and focus by manipulating the visual environment through a mastery of intensity control.

The Importance of Precise Intensity Control

In many theatres today, it is not unusual to have separate control over each outlet in the performance lighting system. In a well designed system, this may translate into individual control of nearly all of the fixtures that are used to light the performance area. Even when selective control is not available and we have to group or "gang" fixtures together, the object is to have the ability to vary intensity in such a way as to focus audience attention where we want it and create visual interest. Often, even when we do have individual fixture control, we will raise or lower the intensity of a set of fixtures, usually grouped by color, because it might look odd and it might not be practical to change them separately. Precise intensity control within a particular look, scene, or cue, however, can mean the difference between lighting that supports the moment or just plain illumination. Let's refer to our Lighting Key and begin our exploration of intensity control and the resulting changes in light and shadow on the stage.

Using Context to Establish the Overall Lighting Scheme

Once we have identified the sources, some of the elements that we have to consider in developing the cues for the lighting are: time of day, season, weather, locale, historical period, time span of the play, types of action, style of the production, and emotional content. The other physical elements of the production — such as costumes, makeup, sets, furniture, use of (or lack of) **practicals,** floor color, and floor coverings — also come into play, but these are considerations that should be brought to bear in the development of the Light Key along with season, weather, and emotion.

Let's say the play in our example begins in the early afternoon, when the sun is high and flooding the house with warm light. It is just after midsummer in the eastern part of the United States, so it is hot, the flowers are in full bloom, and the trees are laden with bright green leaves. The action is that of a joyful reunion between an adult daughter and her aging parents in the living room of her childhood home.

Researching Context

In the script, the time of day is typically established for the beginning of a scene, often in the introductory stage directions that appear in italics at the beginning of each act or scene. Although additional direction may be included in the text, we must often look to the dialogue between the characters in order to keep pace with the progression of time throughout the play. Other information that provides us with clues about intensity, direction, and color comes from our experience in the natural world or through research about the quality of light in a particular location. It is important to keep in mind that natural light looks different in various parts of the world and at different times of the year.

Firsthand experience in a certain locale is the best way to gain knowledge about the lighting conditions and how the light "feels," but research can provide us with the information we need if a visit to an exotic location is not practical. Research should include color photographs, but paintings, black and white photographs, drawings, and studies of different art forms and archival records from a particular period and locality can yield very appropriate and accurate results.

Although it is true that a painting is an interpretation of what the artist sees, it often captures the essence of the meaningful qualities of the light, which can actually make some choices more clear for the lighting designer. After all, both at the most basic level and in their highest achievement, paintings are studies in light, shadow, and color. A good example of the range of emotion that can be conveyed through the art of the period would be to compare photographs taken during the Great Depression in the 1930s in the United States and the paintings of Paris in the 1890s. Each of these examples gives a clear representation of the emotional backdrop of the period.

So, if you are lighting a production that takes place in an unfamiliar location, it is important to do some research in order to have a point of reference for the Lighting Key and the overall design. This research often yields valuable information that can be incorporated into other aspects of the design and can indicate a framework for the emotional context of the play.

If the play is a fantasy, or takes place in some unfamiliar place that can't be referenced through research, it is necessary to rely purely on script analysis to create a lighted environment that is appropriate to the production. Also keep in mind that a play doesn't have to take place in some faraway land in order to require lighting that differs from your everyday experience and, conversely, that the natural lighting in some exotic places may be very similar to that in your hometown. Check the globe and compare locations relative to the equator. They often have very similar qualities of light.

All this may seem like a lot of detail, and a great deal of trouble to go through for each scene, but when we combine these elements with the emotional context of the stage action, a road map for the lighting begins to emerge and there is less chance that we will introduce something through the lighting that may confuse the audience.

Determining Initial Intensities

Back to our sample scene: the sun is high and hot and we have the motivation to call for a fairly high level of intensity from the warm-side front light. On this cloudless day, we can also justify using only a slightly lower reading for the cool-side front light. This will reduce the contrast between the intensity from the warm side and the cool side, which will look natural, as we expect a fairly high level of reflected light on a bright day. The trickiest component of this scenario is determining the intensity of the backlight. We are delivering a fairly intense level of front light to the stage, so we have to be sure that we have sufficient backlight on the performers to keep them from blending into the scenery. The problem is that if we use too much backlight, we may introduce that "nighttime" feel to the scene, and the audience will become confused about the time of day without knowing why.

Remember, backlight is only discernable in certain areas, such as on the shoulders and hair, but in these critical areas it doesn't take much to send a confusing message to the audience. Other elements that are noticeably affected by backlight are the floor, floor coverings, and any horizontal furniture surfaces, such as tabletops and the seats of chairs and sofas, particularly if they are light in color. Look to these areas as well when adjusting the backlight. It is often the look of the floor that helps to determine the final intensity setting for these instruments in a particular scene.

Now that we have established the opening look for the show, we have a basis upon which to develop a progression of cues that will carry us through the changes in time, action, and emotion throughout the play. We do this through careful script analysis and attention to detail regarding season, weather, time of day, and emotion. Some find it helpful to develop a chart that tracks all the factors governing the lighting for the entire production. (See figure 6.1 on page 70 for an example.) These charts can be very helpful in identifying the key components of a production and their relative importance. What is revealed in the charts is the cyclic nature of many productions and how the intensity levels of the lighting often correspond with the intensity levels of the emotion. The charts are particularly useful as we develop our craft because they help us identify and track important production elements and they provide a convenient way to map the progression of the lighting through the play. They can also be a place to begin noting the pace of the cuing.

Shifting Focus Using Balance and Contrast

Once we have established the overall look of each scene, we can begin to craft the light in ways that steer the audience to look at certain areas and concentrate their attention on a place that the production team has deemed appropriate. This is where we can begin to apply the true spirit of the Robert Edmond Jones' quote mentioned earlier, in which he says that lighting design is "putting light where you want it and taking it away where you don't." This intentional placement of light is known as changing focus (audience focus, that is) or "pulling focus" to a certain part or parts of the stage. Changing focus involves the adjustment of intensity in one sense, but on a more global level, it is a study in balance and **contrast**. Varying the levels of all the warm-side front lights by exactly the same amount throughout a production may track the time of day accurately and provide adequate illumination for a play, but it does little to focus our attention on a particular person or group. This type of cuing also falls short of supporting the emotional ebb and flow of the production, which is another significant contribution of good lighting design.

The key element that is missing is contrast, the difference between areas of light and areas of shadow. Lack of contrast, whether the scene is too bright or too dark, creates visual fatigue and boredom. As mentioned earlier, we can't go to the other extreme and expect the audience to accept seeing widely varying colors and intensities on a performer as they cross the stage either, at least not in our naturalistic example. We can, however, find opportunities to dim a part (or most) of a room where there isn't any action for a while, shift the color balance in an area where a couple is engaged in a romantic interlude, or pull the general room intensity down while raising the levels on a featured performer who is delivering an important discourse. While successful light variation can be achieved in many ways, the essence of shifting focus is to adjust the **contrast ratio** of the stage picture to achieve the desired result.

Contrast Ratio and Human Perception

Contrast can be defined as the difference between areas that are dark and areas that are bright. Contrast ratio is the difference between the darkest and brightest levels that can be differentiated by a type of film, a television camera, or the human eye. A high contrast ratio indicates that the difference between the brightest and darkest areas is great. Conversely, low contrast ratio means that the difference between the brightest and darkest areas is not that significant. If one part of a photo is twice as bright as another, the contrast ratio is said to be two to one and is expressed as 2:1. If the subject we are studying has an area that is four times as bright as another area, the contrast ratio would be four to one, or 4:1, and so on.

The human eye is capable of responding to an extremely wide range of contrast in a single visual image. Even the most sophisticated television cameras and still and motion picture films fall far short of the human visual system in this respect. Slide film and motion picture film are noted for their ability to mimic the human eye, but in comparison, they quickly develop white "hot spots" that obliterate anything nearby or make objects in the shadows fade into blackness. There are instruments that are capable of measuring very slight differences in light intensity, but there is no tool or collection of instruments that has the ability of the combination of the human eye and brain to respond to, register, interpret, remember, and compare information about the visual environment.

It is important to remember that "seeing" for humans involves a "system" composed of the eye, the connectivity between the eye and the brain, and the brain itself. A normal, healthy eye responds very accurately and predictably and is difficult to fool. Sometimes the connection between the eye and the brain is faulty and creates interference in the reception of the signal, for which there is any number of names for illnesses or conditions. The most subjective and easily fooled part of the system is the brain, and everything we see, we see through the "filters" that have developed in our brain. So we are dealing with a visual system that is unparalleled in its capabilities, but that can also be manipulated in some predictable ways.

One of the most predictable features of the system is that humans will always look to the area of highest perceived brightness. The term *perceived brightness* is used because, as we have seen and will continue to explore, certain colors of light may *seem* less bright even when they are indeed at a higher intensity that an adjacent light of another color. And the qualifier *always* applies unless we specifically train a person or group of people to look to another part of the visual field for important information. This training would have to be performed in isolation, be very intense, and probably be tied to survival in some way. Even if the training were successful, the subjects would quickly revert to the "brightest takes precedence" reaction when returned to normal circumstances. This natural response prevails in our everyday experience and translates easily to the stage.

Adjusting Brightness

Focusing the attention of the audience through the use of brightness is probably the most universal convention that we apply to developing our craft into an artful progression of cues for a production. We can achieve *relative* brightness in one of two ways. We can either increase the intensity of light on a subject or decrease the intensity of the surrounding areas. If all the levels start out the same, we can theoretically achieve the same 2:1 change in contrast ratio by either raising the intensity on the subject by a factor of two *or* by lowering the intensity of the surrounding areas by one half. In reality, the correlation between the high and low intensities may not work out in precisely this manner to produce a *perceived* 2:1 brightness change, but the point is that making one place on the stage look brighter than another does not always involve increasing intensity.

Other factors besides intensity affect our perception of brightness. Typically cool colors, especially blues, seem less bright than warm colors even when identical fixtures are used and they are operating at the same intensity. This has to do with the way our eye receives the light but also with our learned notion that blue light is associated with night, when light levels are lower. Brightness adaptation also comes into play in perceiving brightness, along with the speed of the cues and the direction of the light.

If we wish to create tension in an audience, we can do so by frustrating their desire to see a performer's face, perhaps by making the sky-drop behind them bright and keeping the front light dim. The contrast ratio is high, but the sky is a large, bright blank slate and the audience will still look at the performer to receive important information from his or her face. When a bright area holds no pertinent information for us, our brain treats it as glare and we try to block it out or minimize its effects in order to see the object that is being veiled by the excessive brightness. The audience will keep checking the sky for the slightest change, but if none is perceived, they will increasingly try to focus on the performer, especially if he or she is moving about the stage. We are pitting the normal "brightest takes precedence" response against the desire to see the performer's face, which results in a conflict that will truly make the audience restless and uncomfortable because the conflict cannot be resolved. This type of device should be used on a limited basis and only after being carefully considered. Even then, it should only be used for limited periods of time. Audiences that are made to feel uncomfortable must also feel that there was some justification for the tension, to bring a better understanding the work, or they may not come back.

The adjustments that we make in intensity and contrast ratio in order to focus the attention of the audience are a natural extension of the way that we plan how the light will be controlled when we create the Light Plot, which we will explore in more depth in the chapters that follow.

Creating Mood

Mood is the word that is most closely associated with the "feeling" or the emotion of the moment. Mood can be created in a number of different ways, including the color and direction of the light as well as focus, movement, and intensity.

Different types of productions evoke different styles of approach in the lighting design. Dramas, or "straight plays" as they are sometimes called, are often categorized as either comedies or tragedies. We begin our script analysis with that basic premise and assume a lighting style that usually has a naturalistic character to it. Musicals may have a tragic quality to them but, in general, they are considered a "lighter" form of entertainment. The audience accepts the convention that cast members may break into song at any moment and are willing to engage their "suspension of disbelief" to a greater degree than for a dramatic presentation. Therefore, we start with a different point of reference when we begin thinking about how we will light this type of performance, not only because what is required of the design is vastly different, but also because the themes are geared toward the use of music to play on our emotions. Lavish scores are written for operas, and designers typically adorn them with equally lavish sets, lights, and costumes in keeping with the "heightened sense of reality" portrayed in this genre. Dance productions are based in a unique lighting convention that places the emphasis on side lighting while relying heavily on the mood created by that lighting to help tell the story. Ballet, jazz, modern, ethnic, and interpretive dance can all employ tragic or cheerful themes, often within the context of a single piece. In order to keep pace with shifting themes and the expressive nature of dance, a high degree of attention to detail and thoughtfulness are required on the part of the lighting designer.

In a similar manner to those already mentioned, each type of event, from fashion shows to industrials to rock 'n' roll and award ceremonies, have different requirements in the type, placement, and quantity of instruments, but also in the mood that is set as we anticipate how the audience will react from moment to moment. Here again, this is not to say that there are certain "rules" to follow in lighting each production type. Rather, it is a reminder that production styles develop conventions (that shift from time to time) and more importantly, that we need to be aware of the overall theme of the piece and the emotional variations that can be enhanced through setting the proper mood with the lighting.

Using Intensity and Direction to Create Mood

The mood of the lighting is often thought of as being most closely tied to color when, in reality, it is more dependent on the *intensity* and *direction* of the light. This assertion has to be tempered by the fact that our *perception* of intensity is based, to some degree, on the color of the light. For this next part of our exploration, though, imagine that color filter media does not exist and we are charged with shaping mood through the creative use of the intensity and direction of only white light.

We would all agree that a scene played in light that is set at half the intensity of the preceding scene would seem more somber. Likewise, a scene that is played in light that has areas of more pronounced light and shadow would have more of an "edge" to it, due to the tension created through the higher contrast ratios. Similarly, a scene played in strong high side light would evoke a different level of dramatic tension than the same scene acted out with a higher level of front light. So, when we think about creating mood, we should base our fundamental decisions about how we fashion the mood of a scene in those controllable qualities of light that affect the audience in the most profound ways. Once we have found the best combination of intensity and direction, or angle, for the lighting, we can begin to think about how we can best use color to enhance the feelings we are trying to evoke.

Charting Lighting and Emotional Cycles

Shaping the emotional response of the audience through the lighting can be accurately expressed by the phrase "lighting the emotional life" of the production. Authors of finely crafted scripts usually take the conventions that we use to light particular times of day, the seasons, and location into consideration in order to take advantage of the type of light in which the scene will be played. That is to say that most playwrights will gear the emotional content of a scene to the luminous environment they call for when they establish the parameters of time and place for that scene. A good reason for this is that, just as the seasons and the passage of time are cyclic in nature, so is the emotional framework of a play. The cycle of day to night and back to day will yield a sinusoidal "wave" that is often tracked closely by the shifting waves of emotion. (See figure 6.1. On this chart, the top wave represents fluctuations in the time of day, while the bottom wave represents shifts in emotional intensity.) Most playwrights use this device instinctively, as it is an intrinsic part of human nature.

T.O.D.	12:00 PM	5:00 PM	8:00 PM	10:00 PM	8:00 AM	10:00 AM	12:00 PM	5:00 PM
LIGHT LEVEL	HI	MOD HI	MOD	LOW	MOD HI	HI	HI	MOD HI
COND.	MID SUN	BEGIN SET	EVE	NIGHT MOON	RISE	SUN/ CLOUD	MID SUN	BEGIN SET
EMOTION DESC.	REUNION	QUIET DINNER	CARD GAME	BED TIME	WAKE BKFST	REVEAL GIFT	REVEAL FIANCEE	DEPART
EMOTION LEVEL	HI	MOD	MOD	LOW	HI	HI	HI	MOD HI

Figure 6.1. Time of day/emotion chart

When a chart such as this reveals a conflict between the conventions for correlating the lighting with the emotional content, careful analysis is required in the approach used to light that scene. Often, the contradiction is used to create tension, such as in the nighttime fight scene in *West Side Story,* and it can also be used for dramatic effect, which this scene does so well. Although staging this particular scene at night remains true to the reality of a gang conflict of the period, we have to approach the lighting on the premise that there is tension between low light levels and high emotional content.

Sometimes the dramatic reasons for a contradiction between lighting intensity and emotional intensity are more obscure, but we need to consider what they might be and discover them if we can. If, in conjunction with the director and the rest of the design team, we are unable to identify the dramatic intent of such a contradiction, it may be necessary to find ways to light a scene differently. When we go down this road, however, we must also justify the choices we make and remain true to the intent of the piece's creator. This holds true for all forms of production, from the most delicately crafted love scene (whether in a play or a ballet), to the most outrageous and bawdy "alternative" style of production. By the way, after a while the creation of the chart becomes second nature as a part of the thought process in the analysis of the work at hand, and it is no longer necessary to draw it on paper.

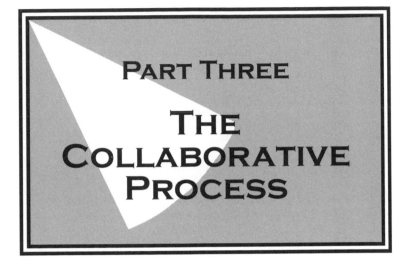

PART THREE

THE COLLABORATIVE PROCESS

Chapter Seven
Communicating the Intent

Up until now, we have been exploring those parts of the design process that can be considered independent or somewhat solitary in nature. This doesn't mean that any designer should ever work in a vacuum. The entire process of design is collaborative, and it begins with the first reading of the script or the analysis of other material, the first look at a dance in the studio, or the first production meeting. Collaboration continues through discussions with the director, conductor, and choreographer, as well as interactions with other members of the design team while examining fabric swatches and painters' elevations. But the development of the lighting design is work that takes place in the mind and studio of the designer, alone with his or her thoughts and special skills, in harmony with the concept for the production that reflects the collective insights of those involved. The lighting designer determines how the lighting will support the production and what it will look like, but now he or she must have the means to document those ideas and possess the skills to effectively communicate them to others. This is done through a series of drawings and other paperwork that accurately depict, among other things, where each instrument is to be located; its type, wattage, and channel assignment; what brand and size of color media is to be cut for it; and how it is to be identified.

Lighting Drawings

The two drawings that are most important to the lighting process are the **Light Plot** and the **Lighting Section**. These drawings were discussed briefly in the beginning chapters but we will take an in-depth look at them now.

The Light Plot

The Light Plot is a plan view of the theatre, drawn to scale, that shows things such as the walls surrounding the stage and audience chamber, the outline of any scenery, the location of the masking, and of course, the lighting instruments on the battens both over the stage and the audience (see figure 7.1). It also shows any additional

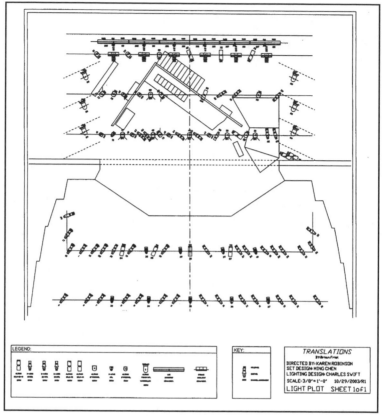

Figure 7.1. Light Plot

lighting positions, such as booms or light ladders on the stage or in the house, and follow spots if the production calls for them. The scale is typically $1/2'' = 1'-0''$ (one half inch equals a foot), but some larger venues can only be represented on a reasonably sized sheet of paper in the smaller $3/8'' = 1'-0''$ scale. Avoid the temptation to use $1/4'' = 1'-0''$ (one quarter inch to the foot) scale because the distance between lighting fixtures will generally be too small to allow the information pertaining to each unit to be included in a legible size. Remember that a plan view is one that shows the theatre as if the roof has been removed and we are viewing the venue from a low-flying helicopter that is directly overhead. The plan view does not indicate the height of the various elements, so we must include those in a textual form on the drawing where necessary — for instance, to call out the **trim heights** of the electrics battens.

The main function of the Plot is to show the stage electricians where each lighting instrument is located on each batten. The different fixture symbols, which are identified in the Legend on the drawing, represent different types of instruments (see figure 7.2). We can add modifications to the standard symbols to indicate variations of a particular type of fixture. Other information that is indicated on the drawing appears in a standard location relative to each lighting instrument symbol, or inside a shape such as a hexagon, circle, or ellipse that is identified in the **Key** (see figure 7.2). We typically want to show instrument type and any accessories, unit number, color number, pattern number, and channel assignment, and leave a place for the dimmer or circuit number to be written in. This is a lot of information, but if it is organized well and placed with a little creativity, it will all fit nicely on the drawing, it will be easy to read, and the drawing will look good as well.

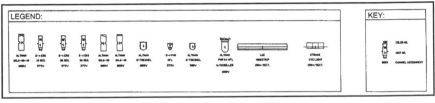

Figure 7.2. Legend and Key for Light Plot

We need to take a little departure here to talk about drawing quality, how the drawings are created, and how to present the information.

Creating the Drawings

THE "OLD" DAYS

Not so long ago learning to become a designer also meant learning to be a draftsman so that you could communicate using the accepted conventions and drawing standards. The first part of drafting was learning the tools (pencils, templates, squares, parallel rules, and the different types of paper) and how to use them. As a designer, you would spend hours learning how to draw a perfectly uniform line with a pencil and straightedge. Of course, this was only possible once you had learned how to properly secure the paper to the drafting table so that it wouldn't shift around while you were trying to draw the Plot on it. Then there was that fateful moment when it was time to peel off the tape that was holding down the drawing without tearing your precious work of art.

Once you had mastered using the tools and acquired a mound of different drawing templates for lighting instruments and set pieces, as well as a pile of generic ones with unique shapes to draw the odd architectural feature when it was required, then came the hard part. It was time to develop and perfect a freehand lettering style that fell within accepted guidelines, was always perfectly legible (even when placed on the drawing at 3:00 or 4:00 AM) and could be put down *fast*. Learning to create accurate, legible, smudge-free, beautiful drawings was a daunting task. Creating the drawing for each show typically meant an all-nighter for the designer, followed by **"the hang"** the next day, and focusing on into that night.

CAD (COMPUTER AIDED DRAFTING)

Thankfully, the days of having to become a draftsman in order to communicate your lighting ideas are, for the most part, gone. This doesn't mean that it's not important to understand what constitutes good drawing practice or that you shouldn't organize your drawings within accepted standards. Today it is still true that the first impression that the crew has of you as a designer, especially if it is a professional crew, is your Light Plot. If the drawing is sloppy and unclear, even if the design is good, you will have to overcome an initial negative impression from the crew. Luckily, with the specialty lighting design drawing programs that are available at affordable prices today, it isn't hard to turn out a great drawing every time. You still have to draw, using a computer as an aid. The learning curve is a bit steep at first, but with the tutorials, tech support, and third-party manuals that are available for most of the programs, along with a little guidance from a knowledgeable friend or colleague, it isn't unheard of for someone with a little CAD (Computer Aided Drafting) experience to be able to turn out a good-looking plot after only a couple of sessions with the design software.

The only actual "drawing" that has to be done is in laying out the plan of the stage and audience chamber, an outline of the set, and of course, the positions of the lighting battens. You never have to worry about drawing a particular fixture correctly, tracing it from a template over and over again, even if you've never seen it. The fixture symbols are selected from a huge library that is part of the design program. The symbols are unique to each fixture type and are accurate scale representations of the manufacturers' products so that when you place or "hang" it on the Plot, you know exactly how much room it takes up. The symbols also have **attributes** (different from robotic fixture attributes, which we will discuss later) assigned to them for all the pertinent information associated with the fixture, such as color number, unit number, channel assignment, and the like. The attribute placeholders for the fixtures and their accessories are located in the proper positions with the correct symbols in and around the instruments. A mouse click and simple edit are all that are required to customize the information for your Plot.

Most of the programs include the ability to accept information regarding the height of set pieces and the surrounding stage walls. Entering this information and associating it with the lines in the plan view enables the program to generate a section view, a front and rear elevation, and in most cases, a three-dimensional rendering that can be looked at from a number of view points. The plan view or Light Plot is typically the only drawing that other people see because it is the one that locates all of the instruments.

The Lighting Section

Another drawing that is usually seen only by the designer but that is vital to the success of a lighting design is the Lighting Section. To review, this is the drawing that represents what we

would see if we took a giant saw and cut down through the theatre on the centerline from front to back (see figure 7.3) The Section is the drawing we look to in order to determine the angle of incidence from the lighting fixtures to the stage.

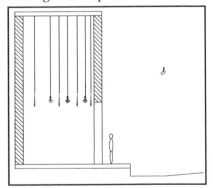

The importance of the Section cannot be stressed enough; it is required in order to achieve a successful design, even if you are the only one

Figure 7.3. Lighting Section

who sees it. The reason the Section is so important is that it helps us to think of the light as a three-dimensional entity, it clearly indicates correct or incorrect angles of incidence, it identifies interferences, and it is the only way to accurately determine throw distance. Many otherwise good designs, even those done by experienced designers, have failed when put into the theatre because the designer didn't take the time to do a section drawing. You do not want to fall victim to the idea that once the Plot is done the design is done.

Even when using a design program to generate the Plot, it's not a bad idea to start off with an accurate hand drawn Section to get an idea of where the battens are located relative to the architecture, performance area, and set pieces. The key here is accuracy. The battens must be properly located in space in order for the Section to serve a useful purpose. This can be difficult when you are designing for a theatre that you have never visited and the tech director only has a plan available. This happens less and less because most theatres have taken steps to make CAD drawings available to designers, but in a pinch, a call to the theatre can usually result in obtaining very accurate heights for the fixed electrics relative to the stage floor.

Obviously, the Lighting Section is also vital in determining trim heights for the stage electrics, which are then noted on the Plot. Dimensions relating to height are given using the stage floor as the 0'-0" reference. Most of the computer drawing programs for lighting designers prompt you for height information for the electrics, which must be entered before continuing the drawing session. The beauty of this is that once you have completed the Plot you can view a Section drawing simply by selecting a different tab in the drawing file, and you can print out the Section for reference.

It's "easy" for the computer to create the Section drawing without doing a lot of extra work, because it is continually tracking all the coordinates in the Plot, along with the height information about the battens. You can use the Section to check the angle of incidence for front and backlight and then switch to an elevation view to check side light angles. Also, once the instruments have been "hung" properly on the electrics in the computer plan view (Light Plot), we can use the "focus" function to direct them to their assigned positions on the stage. When we do this and also enter a number for the color attribute, the program will represent the beam of light in the exact color we have chosen. If the design program has three-dimensional rendering capabilities, the beams of light will not only appear in the proper color, but they will also look elliptical on the stage floor on the computer model, just as they do in the theatre. The beams will be the proper size for the throw distance, and if we have placed a pattern in the unit (i.e., chosen from the pattern or **gobo** library), the pattern will be displayed accurately in the selected color as well. The computer does much of the repetitive drawing work, but the designer still has to make the choices.

Selecting and Learning a Drawing Program

Choosing a design drawing program can be challenging. The successful ones have the same basic features and are specifically designed to output lighting-related documents, but each is written in a different way, and the simplest functions can have very different approaches. Ask around and see which programs have the best features, are the most intuitive, and have the best tech support. You may get some varied opinions, but a few programs will be mentioned over and over again, and you can make your choice based on the features that are most appealing to you. Ask about current prices too. After you learn the program, you will need to purchase and register a licensed copy of the software and own a computer powerful enough to run it on. It wouldn't make too much sense to learn a program and then not have access to it.

It can be challenging to learn how to draw on a computer and master the ins and outs of a lighting program while trying to get a show done on a tight schedule. The best way to learn a CAD design program is to take a class. These are specialized classes, typically offered in college curricula, but they are also available through the software developers and various theatre arts related organizations. If training in a specific type of lighting design program is unavailable, look into courses that offer training in one of the CAD drawing programs. These are typically offered at community colleges and are within driving distance of most small cities and towns. Larger metropolitan areas often have several municipal and private educational facilities that offer classes over a wide range of scheduled times and skill levels.

Once you master the drawing skills in a particular style of CAD program, you can select a design program that is based on that drawing software. It helps to have an idea what lighting design program you would ultimately like to use and will be able to afford so that you can become adept at using the drawing software upon which your desired lighting design program is based. It also helps to know how to draw using a computer first, but even if you do know how, it is important to have someone to help you through the process of learning the design program. The programs are very powerful, to the point of sometimes being overwhelming, and the commands and sequences used to perform a function using one brand of software may be totally different from another, even though some of the command *names* are exactly the same. Having someone who uses the software regularly to guide you through the process *greatly* reduces the frustration level when you are trying one of these programs for the first time. With a little help in the beginning, it's not too hard to master the basic skills in a few sessions.

Other Advantages to CAD Based Lighting Design

The power and convenience of the CAD based lighting design programs go much further than generating clean, accurate, scale drawings. The programs also have "Report" functions that generate all the associated paperwork that used to take hours of additional time for the designer to produce. The information for the various reports is taken directly from the Plot because all the information is resident there. Location and focus information are tracked whenever we place or "hang" and then "focus" a fixture, and the other information, such as color and channel, is selected from the "Attributes" tables, which we edit to suit our particular purpose. Without a design program, it was an arduous task to hand letter all the information for each entry for every fixture in the Plot, even if you had a spreadsheet program to generate blank forms for the Instrument Schedule. With a computer and design software, it's simply a matter of choosing the way you want a particular set of information displayed. Once the design is done, you select the "Report" function in the program and choose the report that is appropriate. In a matter of minutes you can print out an Instrument Schedule, Channel Hook-Up, Shop Order (an equipment list, by fixture type, for rentals) and the always-exciting Color Cut List. Here again, it's easy to extract this information from the plot because when you "placed" the color in the unit (by changing the attribute code) a record of that information was created, including the frame and color size required for each instrument. All of the information is coordinated, it's clear and legible, it has the correct show title and production team names, and it can be printed with your custom logo to boot.

The final advantage to computer aided design programs is that all the design documents, including the drawings, can be transmitted virtually anywhere, electronically, in a matter of seconds. As the ability to share drawings between designers and venues becomes more and more of a necessity, the viability of drawing by hand will continue to diminish. Designers must still understand good drafting technique, and follow the conventions and drawing standards that make up acceptable drawing practice. Also keep in mind that it is not up to the computer to design the lighting or to make all the decisions about how the drawings will look. It is still up to the designer to know what equipment to use and where to place it and how to lay out the drawings in a logical, organized, and creative manner. With the aid of the design software, however, we are free to spend more time on the *design* and less time on the drafting and paperwork.

Lighting Paperwork

The paperwork that accompanies the design drawing(s) is vital to obtaining a properly executed design. The Light Plot does contain most of the essential information, but it is not represented on the drawing in a way that is advantageous for all the different operations that have to be carried out in conjunction with hanging the fixtures. Although there are many standard reports that can be generated using one of the CAD lighting design programs, and custom ones that can be created, we will look at only a few that will be common for most productions.

Instrument Schedule

First is the Instrument Schedule (see figure 7.4 for an example of an Instrument Schedule for the E2 position). This is a spreadsheet-style document that contains most of the information that is on the Plot along with some additional information. The Instrument Schedule is a list of all the fixtures, typically sorted by position starting with the Front-of-House, that shows the fixtures in numerical order from one end of the batten, boom, or ladder to the other. The numbering should start at "1" for each position, which means, for example, that the first instrument on the second house electric would show up as 2H-1. The third fixture on the first onstage electric would be E1-3 and so on. Traditional Instrument Schedules would also list, for each fixture, things such as the channel number, dimmer or circuit number, wattage, color number, frame size, pattern number, purpose, focus, ganging information, and notes.

The Instrument Schedule is used to arrange the information from the Plot in a convenient form, which alleviates the need for everyone to carry a blueprint of the Plot around with him or her. Before CAD design programs, however, it served another important function even before anyone but the designer saw it. It was used by designers to check their work, particularly the numbering, on the Plot before having the blueprints made. If an instrument was deleted or moved for some reason and the unit numbering for the instruments hung on that lighting position didn't get changed, it would be easy to pick that out on the Instrument Schedule and then make the correction on the drawing. Channel or color assignments

Instrument Schedule (All Layers) 5/28/2004 21:25

Venue: STILLWELL THEATRE Show: TRANSLATIONS
Designer: C. SWIFT Assistant: B. TILLY

E2

Unit	Channel	Patch	Dimmer	Type	Lens	Wattage	Purpose	Colour	Gobo
1	59			CE Source 4	26 Degree	575	BENCH BACK	R02	
2	69			Altman Stage Lighting 175 8" Fresnel		1000	U.L. RAIN	R88	
3	61			CE Source 4	26 Degree	575	MID L TREES	R62	G579
4	60			CE Source 4	26 Degree	575	MID L TREES	R87	G579
5	83			Altman Stage Lighting 1KL6-40		1000	RED LOFT	R120	
6	53			Altman Stage Lighting 175 8" Fresnel		1000	L	R62 & BD	
7	52			Altman Stage Lighting 175 8" Fresnel		1000	K	R74 & BD	
8	46			Altman Stage Lighting 165 6" Fresnel		750	P	R08	
9	45			Altman Stage Lighting 165 6" Fresnel		750	K	R08 & BD	
10	78			Altman Stage Lighting 175 8" Fresnel		1000	DOOR MOON	R62	
11	77			Altman Stage Lighting 175 8" Fresnel		1000	DOOR DAY	R08 & BD	
						9225			

Figure 7.4. Instrument Schedule (E2, second electric)

could sometimes get out of whack in the wee hours of the morning, and the Instrument Schedule was a good crosscheck for that too. The Instrument Schedule is still used by most designers to check all this information, but now it is more a check for typos than anything else, because the information on the Schedule that is generated by a design program is derived from the fixture attributes on the Plot. There is little chance for deviation between the two; it's just sometimes easier to pick up mistakes by looking at the paperwork rather than the drawing.

Color Cut List

Another document that is essential on the day of the hang is the "cut list" for the color (see figure 7.5). Typically, a stage electrician will be sent off to the "gel room" to gather all the color for the show and secure it in the proper size frames. The electrician will usually

82

pull the available color, cut any additional pieces needed, and then use the Instrument Schedule to place the color in frames, laying them out in separate stacks for each lighting position. This can be a two- or three-hour task for even a "small" show if the designer provides a good cut list.

The days of the **Master Electrician** taking the time to generate the cut list from the Plot are all but gone because, once the color attributes for each fixture have been entered into a CAD lighting design program, a cut list is little more than a mouse click away. For each fixture the designer selects, the program generates the proper dimensions for the color based on the information stored in the database. This is another handy feature of computer based design programs, especially if you do

Colour Count		(All Layers)		5/28/2004 21:30
Venue:	STILLWELL THEATRE	**Show:**	TRANSLATIONS	
Designer:	C. SWIFT	**Assistant:**	B. TILLY	

Colour	Type	Count
000	6.25" Colour Frame	1
R02	6" Colour Frame	4
R02	6.25" Colour Frame	1
R08	10" Colour Frame	2
R08	6.25" Colour Frame	2
R08	7.5" Colour Frame	6
R09	6.25" Colour Frame	14
R13	6" Colour Frame	1
R16	3.5" x 4.75" Colour Frame	30
R51	6" Colour Frame	1
R55	6.25" Colour Frame	2
R62	10" Colour Frame	2
R62	6.25" Colour Frame	4
R63	10" Colour Frame	1
R63	6" Colour Frame	1
R65	7.5" Colour Frame	9
R67	6" Colour Frame	1
R68	7.5" Colour Frame	1
R74	10" Colour Frame	7
R87	6.25" Colour Frame	4
R88	10" Colour Frame	2
R120	10" Colour Frame	1
R120	3.5" x 4.75" Colour Frame	30
R120	6" Colour Frame	3
R120	Coda Colour Frame	6
R121	Coda Colour Frame	6
R122	3.5" x 4.75" Colour Frame	30
R125	Coda Colour Frame	6
R355	6.25" Colour Frame	14

Figure 7.5. Color Cut List

a lot of touring work and may be working with unfamiliar equipment that has a frame size that you don't happen to know. Some of the frame sizes in the TV and movie industries vary by minute increments among similar fixtures made by the same manufacturer. As long as the information in the database is accurate, the designer no longer needs to worry. You can also use the fixture library to look up fixture information that you may need.

Channel Hookup

Another piece of paperwork that takes on greater significance later in the production process is the Channel Hookup or Channel Schedule (see figure 7.6). The Channel Hookup is used by the designer and then by the Master Electrician and the **Stage Manager** to check each fixture before a rehearsal or a performance. Traditionally called a *dimmer check,* the terminology has evolved with the advent of remotely controlled dimming systems to *channel check.* The former term is still in wide use, however, and will probably remain in the lighting vocabulary for some time to come.

The Channel Hookup typically contains all of the information that is shown on the Instrument Schedule; it is just arranged differently. The Channel Hookup is arranged in ascending channel

Channel Schedule

(All Layers)

5/28/2004 21:27

Venue: STILLWELL THEATRE
Designer: C.SWIFT

Show: TRANSLATIONS
Assistant: B. TILY

Channel	Dimmer	Patch	Purpose	Focus	Type	Lens	Position	Unit	Colour	Gobo
1			A		CE Source 4	26 Degree	1H	21	R355	
2			B		CE Source 4	19 Degree	2H	18	R355	
3			C		CE Source 4	19 Degree	2H	15	R355	
4			D		CE Source 4	19 Degree	2H	12	R355	
5			E		CE Source 4	19 Degree	2H	11	R355	
6			F		CE Source 4	19 Degree	2H	19	R355	
7			G		CE Source 4	19 Degree	2H	17	R355	
8			H		CE Source 4	19 Degree	2H	14	R355	
9			A		CE Source 4	19 Degree	2H	9	R09	
10			B		CE Source 4	19 Degree	2H	8	R09	
11			C		CE Source 4	19 Degree	2H	5	R09	
12			D		CE Source 4	19 Degree	2H	2	R09	
13			E		CE Source 4	26 Degree	1H	1	R09	
14			F		CE Source 4	19 Degree	2H	6	R09	
15			G		CE Source 4	19 Degree	2H	3	R09	
16			H		CE Source 4	19 Degree	2H	1	R09	
17			J		CE Source 4	19 Degree	1HL	2	R355 & TH	
18			K		CE Source 4	19 Degree	1H	20	R355 & TH	
19			L		CE Source 4	19 Degree	1H	16	R355 & TH	
20			M		CE Source 4	19 Degree	1H	13	R355 & TH	
21			N		CE Source 4	19 Degree	1H	22	R355 & TH	
22			P		CE Source 4	19 Degree	1H	19	R355 & TH	
23			J		CE Source 4	19 Degree	1H	10	R09	
24			K		CE Source 4	19 Degree	1H	6	R09	

Figure 7.6. Channel Schedule

order, regardless of fixture type or location, and a single channel may include multiple instruments. The channels follow the (hopefully) logical sequence of control assignments that the designer has chosen for a particular production in a particular venue. We will look at the differences between dimmer and channel assignments and channel logic in more depth in an upcoming chapter, but for now it's sufficient to say that channels are usually assigned beginning with the Front-of-House positions and ending with the sky or special effects.

THE CHANNEL OR DIMMER CHECK

The habit of performing a dimmer check was originally developed when lamp life was rarely expected to be greater than 200 hours and replacing at least one or two lamps was almost a nightly chore. One of the most important reasons for performing a channel check is often overlooked, however. The channel or dimmer check is not only to see that each instrument will produce light, but also to be sure that the focus for every unit is correct. There are numerous reasons why focus may change: the heating and cooling cycle of the light, color and lamp replacement, and maintenance on an adjoining fixture to name a few. The designer instinctively checks the focus when running through the channels before rehearsal, but the need to consider focus may escape some observers who are members of the production crew. Perhaps this is the reason why more and more "channel checks" are done by bringing all the channels up to 30 percent and looking around to see if all the lights are on. Not only is this not a good way to check for "lamp outs" (because it's just too easy to overlook a single dark fixture in even a small Plot), but also it is obviously impossible for anyone, including the designer, to check fixture focus in this manner.

The objective of the dimmer or channel check is to view the fixture or fixtures associated with a particular channel *individually* to see if they are operating and to verify that the focus intended by the designer has been maintained. The job of communicating these responsibilities to the Stage Manager or the Master Electrician falls to the designer if such tasks have been overlooked in their training. At least verify that it is understood what constitutes a proper channel check as far as you, the designer, are concerned. It may require some on-the-spot training on your part, but it is essential to maintaining the look that you designed for the show.

Typically, an experienced Stage Manager will be able to check the acting areas, practicals, sky, and **"spiked"** specials without a problem. When a show is scheduled for an extended run, or if certain fixtures have a critical focus that is difficult to describe, the designer may also be required to leave behind a "focus plot," complete with illustrations, to help ensure that the focus will be maintained properly. Depending on the production, the difference between proper and improper focus could be determined by increments of less than an inch. The point here is that, just as when the designer begins the focusing process, the fact that the light comes on and has the correct color in it is not enough — it also has to be pointed in the right place — and someone has to be responsible for that during the entire run of the show.

Now that we have taken some time to examine how critical it is to achieve and maintain a good focus, let's take a look at what that means.

Chapter Eight
Focus: The Rush to Perfection

In lighting, the term **focus,** from the electricians' point of view, means to point or aim each lighting instrument to a place on the stage that has been determined by the lighting designer, to lock the unit into place both horizontally and vertically, to make adjustments to the beam as permitted through the features of the fixture or attached accessories, and finally, to place the selected color into the frame holder on the front of the unit. Focus responsibilities for the designer include patience, performing a channel check for lamp operation and correctness of the **patch** *before* beginning the actual focus work, patience, standing in the correct place on the stage to focus the instrument that is on, patience, asking for the intended beam sharpness or size, patience, calling for shutter cuts and looking around and behind you to see where the light beam is going and if it's lighting something that you don't want it to, and patience. This must all be performed as fast as humanly possible, with absolute perfection and with the utmost patience and decorum. This is a challenging time for the designer, the crew, and the entire company, so let's take a look at how to approach the process in a way that achieves the desired result without undue hardship on the cast, crew, and the rest of the production team.

Acquiring Stage Time

The focus procedure generally takes place after the lights are hung and just before "tech week" starts. It marks the first time in the production sequence that "stage time" is devoted to lighting activities alone. But does it ever really happen that lighting is the only thing going on in the theatre at that time? Rarely, but that is the intent. Other activities that do take place during focus are extremely limited due to the fact that all of the lights, except the one that is being focused at the time, are off. It is not uncommon for the size of the carpenter crew to be increased for this **call** so that one carpenter can hold a flashlight on the task at hand while another completes the work.

This is a dangerous practice, however, and space should be scheduled so that other activities can take place elsewhere during the **focus call**. *Under no circumstances* should performers be allowed to rehearse on the stage during focus. If the director insists that the performers have the stage, it is up to the designer to ask for the work lights, break the crew, and come back later to complete the focus. This may sound unreasonable, and the urge is to carry on, but the risk to the performers is simply too high to continue.

If the competing activity can only be carried out in the theatre or on the stage, such as rigging, painting the stage floor, or cleaning the audience chamber, a compromise must be reached and one crew will usually wind up with a late night call. There are some tricks to help work around the demand for stage time during focus, but the plan should be that the stage is devoted exclusively to electrics for the allotted time. With some experience, it is possible to leave a "glow" of light on the stage so the crew members can move around safely, but the glow has to be shifted around the stage such that the low light level doesn't interfere with the focus of a particular instrument.

Focus Duties

Focusing lighting fixtures is a collaborative effort and requires concentration on the part of the designer, the electrician at the light, and the board operator. The designer must come mentally prepared to focus the show precisely in one pass through the plot and, if at all possible, should have the **focus points** spiked on the stage before the crew arrives. The designer must also provide all the necessary updated drawings and paperwork for the show, with enough copies for everyone who needs one and a spare or two.

The electricians must come appropriately dressed for the occasion (including the proper footwear for climbing) and with the correct tools (a wrench, a circuit and lamp tester, and possibly gloves), but without a lot of extra equipment that may restrict movement or end up falling to the stage floor. Electricians also need to bring a good working knowledge of the instruments with which they will be working; they must have the ability to change a lamp quickly if necessary and the willingness to bring an instrument that is "being difficult" into position and lock it there.

The board operator has to remain alert and attentive to requests from the designer and the electrician on the light, as well as knowing the board well enough to perform a patch or switch into dimmer mode to check a circuit. It is also beneficial for the board operator to be able to anticipate the next channel that will be called, the last channel that was up, and the channel numbers for groups of multiple fixtures on a particular electric.

The Focus Procedure

The process for carrying out the focus is simple but sometimes misunderstood. Instruments are focused starting at one end of a hanging position and working across to the other end. Specials are focused as they are encountered in the order and are not focused at a later time. The electrics are focused in this fashion for the convenience of the electricians who are at the lights. It wastes time if they have to run back and forth along the lighting gallery and is even more wasteful and impractical when it comes to the stage electrics. Sometimes, due to the way a particular part of the theatre is constructed, it may be difficult to access fixtures on one end of a lighting position without running the risk of knocking the others out of focus, so the order must be chosen wisely. Focus typically starts at the farthest Front-of-House position, moving closer to the stage, and then from the first onstage electric moving upstage. It is customary to take at least a short break when the transition is made from the house electrics to the stage. It gives everyone a moment to regroup and allows the board operator and focusing electrician to trade places if that is their arrangement.

For the designer, this focusing procedure makes it a little harder to follow the flow of the plot (it's like shooting a movie out of sequence), but it does save *a lot* of time. For the board operator, it means that the channel numbers may be called out of sequence, so, if the board operator can follow along on the Plot or Instrument Schedule and anticipate the next channel, he or she can load it into the board and have it ready to go, again saving time.

Sighting the Hot Spot

Designers use a number of different methods to get the "hot spot" of each light in the right place, such as wearing shades or looking through welding glass directly into the lens of the fixture to center the glow of the filament in the lens. Repeatedly staring into lighting fixtures can cause eye damage, however, even when the fixtures are not run up to full. By far, the best way to focus is to fix your eye on a point at the back of the theatre and have the unit adjusted until you feel that the heat from the instrument is greatest on your face. This takes some practice, and it is hard to resist the temptation to look into the fixture lens, but it is faster and yields a better focus.

Regardless of the method you use to sight the hot spot, it is imperative that the color be removed from a unit before you attempt to focus it, and then inserted when you are satisfied that the focus for each fixture is correct. Sometimes, the **electrics crew** will "drop the color," at least in the house electrics, during the hang to insure they have the color in the right places and all the color has been cut properly. This practice usually saves time, but attempting to focus with the color in typically yields poor results and at least some of the units require refocusing, which eats up more precious stage time.

Completing a Smooth, Efficient Focus

Once the focus starts, the all-important patience factor has to be added to combat the urge to rush through the focus just to get it done. Speeding through this important procedure usually results in a sloppy focus that has to be touched up repeatedly during tech week when the time crunch is greatest. There are numerous reasons why the fixture that you want to focus isn't coming up. It could be a blown lamp (even though it was just checked), it could be a wire that became disconnected because it hasn't been dressed or tied down yet, there might be a tripped circuit breaker or a bad dimmer, the blackout button may have been accidentally pressed, or the grand master on the board may be at zero. Whatever the case, becoming angry about it or yelling at the electricians will not get the light to come on. It is best for the designer to suggest a logical troubleshooting sequence to assist in finding the problem. Many other types of difficulties can be encountered and it's best to try to find a way to deal with the problem and carry on. If you must skip a unit, do so and write a note to return to it later. The main thing is to stay cool and not sacrifice the focus in order to simply get done.

The burden for completing a good, fast focus does not rest solely on the designer. The electricians also bear some of the responsibility, and they can be an important part of achieving the desired results in a reasonable amount of time. The person at the light has a unique view of the light beam and the stage. They are typically at a higher angle and can notice spill or an off-center hot spot more easily than the designer. By advising the designer of an errant spot of light or an instrument that is out of alignment, they can speed up the process and enhance the results.

When the board is brought into the house for focus, the board operator is the only member of the focus team that has the same view of the stage that the audience will have, and he or she can provide valuable input. Even when the board is in the booth, the operator has an overview of the theatre that can help to make additional visits to the fixtures unnecessary if used to advise the designer of something that doesn't look right or may be distracting to the audience.

The electrician and the board operator need to be patient with the designer too. Other designers or the Stage Manager may come in to ask questions or to work out scheduling issues. When this happens, it is up to the designer to ask for a glow onstage and ensure that the next instrument to be focused is not allowed to sit at a high intensity and heat up while the conversation ensues. Hopefully, the designer will be able to keep interruptions brief and the work can continue.

When a group of instruments has been focused (perhaps the downstage warm and cool front lights), take time to check their focus collectively, the way that they will be used in the show. Look for holes or slight variations in the upstage or downstage location of the hot spot and touch them up if need be.

You may find that company members will want to wander onstage from time to time or sit in the house and watch part of the focusing process. A sense of excitement may begin to flow through the company, and with good reason. Keep in mind that, with the possible exception of a few members of the design team, the only person who knows what the lighting is going to look like is you. The electricians get to share a somewhat disjointed preview of the show as the focus continues, but only you know how all the pieces are supposed to come together. If everyone involved in the focus stays alert and works as a team, the focus can be done well, quickly, and only once. Once the focus is done, you can get down to the serious business of writing the cues.

Chapter Nine
Writing Cues

The essence of cue writing can best be described as "expressing the flow of the visual context of the show in a sequence of numbers." This may sound like a procedure that is ill suited to the task of trying to express emotion through lighting , but like Light Plots and paperwork, writing cues is the means by which we can accurately transform the lighting that we see in our minds to the lighting that appears on the stage.

It is interesting to note that, although the tools that we use to execute the lighting continue to evolve, the process remains relatively unchanged. We have to get the ideas that we have about the lighting out of our head and into a form that others can use. We want to have a way to document the lighting changes in the show in order to establish how the show looks *and* to have a way to duplicate those looks as well as the transitions between them.

Documenting Lighting Changes for Repeatability

For the audience, live entertainment is about the interactions onstage and the connection to the work through the performers. There is also the expectation that the show will remain consistent over multiple performances. For the performers and the production staff, it is all about *repeatability.* This is not a dry robot-like approach, but more a search for a method to *re*-create a fresh performance each night that maintains the consistency required to be true to the work and support the company in presenting the show in a way that it is in keeping with the intent. In other words, once the show is "set" in the final days of rehearsal, it should stay relatively the same for its entire run. Adjustments may be made for changes in the cast or to correct a problem that develops during the run, but the audience that sees the show on opening night will expect to see the same show at performance number one hundred or number one thousand, sometimes years later, and down to the smallest detail.

The playwright and the director have the right to expect this as well. This all points to the fact that, since the time when chandeliers laden with candles were lowered into place or candles were snuffed and relit to change the lighting, someone has been charged with the responsibility of remembering or documenting when and how those changes are to take place.

With the advent of more sophisticated forms of lighting, the need to document the settings and changes has become increasingly important to the successful re-creation of the show. In the days of resistance dimmers and **autotransformer** boards, many operators were sometimes required, and each had a set of cue sheets documenting the adjustments for the bank of dimmers for which he or she was responsible. Computers are well suited to the task of recording and "playing back" number sequences, so they are an ideal platform upon which to base the control of lighting systems. Today, when we enter the channel levels and fade times for each cue into a computer console, we are replicating the process that has been used for years, only in a way that is much more accurate and repeatable. The thing to remember is that we are creating the "lighting environment" for the production and the sequencing of numbers is merely the process through which we can document and repeat it.

The Evolution of the Cues

Cues evolve through a process of several steps that can take on a number of different forms depending on production circumstances. The level of production (be it amateur, educational, professional, or somewhere in between), the type of show: (play, musical, dance, or industrial), the circumstances (regular season, repertory, or summer stock), and the personalities within the design team all have an influence on exactly how the process is carried out. Whatever the details of the process, they should all result in a production that is appropriately and well lit.

The best time to begin writing the cues is after the show has been focused and you have a better idea of what the lighting looks like with the set, what's working as expected in terms of the lighting and what may need some adjustment. Typically, only production schedules in academic situations would allow enough time for this, provided that the set is complete. Cue writing actually begins much earlier in the design process, so let's take a look at it from the start.

First Reading

When we read a play, we imagine the action, the locale, the season, the characters, the setting, and the lighting as we read. Those images are the beginnings of analyzing, understanding, and designing the play. The same can be true for music and dance performances. Even if a dance is to be performed without music, the movements that we see in the studio for the first time are initially transformed into a finished piece in our mind. We begin to form the framework of the design, including the cuing, at our first exposure to the work to be lit.

The Production Meeting: Establishing a Concept

Forming preliminary images for a production is part of the analysis of the work. The analysis also should include an initial production meeting with the other members of the artistic team during which ideas are explored and a concept or theme for the production is established. This doesn't mean that every question will be answered or that all decisions that are made at the meeting are set in stone. It means that an artistic vision for the production has been expressed and some parameters for the show have been identified.

Usually the meeting identifies things that do *not* work for the show more clearly than things that do. These points are brought out in statements such as "You will never see the color (fill in the blank) onstage in this show" from the costumer; "You always see (fill in the blank) style windows for the house in this show, but I think I have something that works better" from the set designer; "We will not be doing any (fill in the blank) steps in this production" from the choreographer; or "We're not going to treat the appearance of the (fill in the blank) in the way that other productions have" from the director. These are ways of narrowing the set of endless possibilities that come with the inception of the production process. On the other hand, some very specific information may come out of these discussions, including colors for paint and lights, hardware for the doors on the set, the smallest details of an important prop, or the documenting of a step-by-step procedure for how an actor will be moved on or off stage by a piece of stage machinery.

The key to successful production meetings is to come prepared by being familiar with the work, have some ideas about how your design will support the expression of the work, and *participate* in the discussions that ensue. The topic doesn't have to be lighting in order for your input to be valuable. The direction that the artistic team is taking may not be considering an important production element. A simple statement such as "Wouldn't the window have to be here in order for us the see the moonlight on the actor's face when he's on the bed upstage left?" can help to define the space and may solve a number of other problems, including the difficult chore of getting light on a actor's face when the set is arranged in a manner that doesn't allow it. The idea is not to argue only for those things that will make your efforts to light the stage easier, but to contribute to an overall concept that supports the collective artistic expression and work of others as well. Obviously, if the laws of physics (like light traveling in a straight line) are being ignored, you have to point that out, but understanding and compromise are a big part of the design process for everyone. Express your ideas, have research and materials to support them, but don't get caught up in the notion that your initial impressions of how a production should be lit are all correct and appropriate. You may change your mind before the process is over.

COMMUNICATING EFFECTIVELY

Keep in mind also that the topics of discussion are mainly about the *visual* aspects of the show but they are being expressed *verbally*. This requires mastering verbal imagery on a level that many visual artists may find difficult to achieve. This often proves frustrating for everyone involved.

One of the best ways to overcome the verbal barrier, both in the expression and the understanding of an idea, is to use photographs and sketches. An object that represents a metaphor for the production can also help to bring clarity to the discussions. A metaphor can be defined as a figure of speech in which a word or phrase that ordinarily means one thing is used for another thing in order to suggest a likeness between the two. The distinction between a metaphor and a simile is that a metaphor does not use *like* or *as* in expressing the connection. "This play is a river" is a metaphor. Arriving at a metaphor is generally more challenging than developing a simile, but it is more accurate and rewarding as well because of the more demanding thought process required to find that thing that *is* the play and not something that is *like* the play.

Remember that having a great idea about the lighting is sometimes not enough. You have to be able to express that idea in ways that others can understand, or it may be lost simply through lack of understanding, not because it is without merit. Because directors are more based in the verbal aspects of production (that's why they're directors — they learn better and express themselves better through words), they are notorious for their inability to visualize. Designers are typically visual learners and express themselves best through something that is seen. These differences can set up a communication "barrier" that at times results in bitter disputes over a production element that both director and designers understand in exactly the same way, only neither can express their understanding in a way the other can comprehend. If that sounds confusing, it's meant to, because it is. The point is that we know that the visual-verbal communication deficiencies exist, and we can remedy the situation by anticipating them and bringing materials to help express our ideas. Try it; it really works well and can relieve a lot of the tension that can accompany these initial meetings.

Developing the Plot and Paperwork

Once we have the collaborative concept ironed out, we venture back into a more solitary aspect of designing — thinking about the Plot and the paperwork, where we continue to solidify our ideas about the cuing. Before the Plot and paperwork portion of the work is done, however, there is another collaborative element that comes into play that is not only vitally important but also enjoyable for the designer. You get to break the monotony of carrying the show around in your head and hearing your voice deliver the lines by going to rehearsal.

Attending Rehearsals

Attending rehearsals is one of the most important elements of design, and it is key to writing the cues. Unfortunately, this practice is so underrated and neglected by many designers that most directors hardly expect it anymore. If we look at the process and purpose of attending rehearsals, the significance to the design should become apparent.

The main idea to keep in mind when bringing a play (or other production) to the stage is that plays are *not* created when the script is written, they are *not* created during a read-through, they are *not* created in the director's mind, and they are *not* merely the visual expression of the designers. *Plays are created during rehearsals.* The only way that the words on a page can be brought to life is through the interaction of the actors and the director as they explore not only the words and actions, but also the meanings of the script. Even if you are working on a show that you have done before, *this* production will be unique, *this* production will be established in its own context, and it is important that you attend the rehearsals for *this* production. Even if you are working with the world's most efficient Stage Manager who sends you endless pages of rehearsal notes, an entrance could be changed or a cue line might be altered and you might miss the notation. However, the importance of attending rehearsals goes beyond writing a cue for an upstage entrance that has been changed to a downstage one and avoiding embarrassment at first tech.

EMOTION AND TIMING

Two elements that are vital to the success of the cuing and the overall design can only be observed with this cast enacting this director's interpretation of the work. Those two elements are the *feeling* and the *timing* of each moment in the production.

Earlier, we looked at lighting "the emotional life of the play," where we began to incorporate the proper lighting instruments in the plot to achieve certain "looks." But it is only when we see those moments played out by the actors that we can begin to finalize our ideas about how we can enhance the *feeling* of the moment through lighting. We can then take our rehearsal notes and transform them into the cues that are appropriate for each moment.

The other element that develops through the director's insights and the creative participation of the actors is the *timing* of individual events and the show in general. This is information that we can only discover through the rehearsal process. It is subject to change and requires close attention by the designer. Subtle changes in the duration of a gesture, how a gesture is made, the length of a pause, or the length of time an actor is taking to deliver a line or exit the stage all have an affect on how the cues associated with those activities are executed. Often, the timing between a line or action and the lighting is so critical that a sequence will be run over and over again until the line or action is clearly defined and "set" and the lighting has been adjusted to match it perfectly. Whether we realize it or not, all of the cuing and all of the action of the play are tied together in this way, or they should be. We will intuitively change the time of a cross fade by a count or two so that it "feels" right when it takes place in real time with the actors onstage. These small, routine adjustments to the timing of the cues begin to hint at how closely related the lighting is to the action and emotion of the play. The significance of this relationship should not be overlooked or downplayed at any point in the process.

PACE

Not only do we begin to discern the timing for specific cues during the rehearsal process, but we can also start to form the general framework for the pace of the show. The pace or tempo of a scene is generally faster for more lighthearted moments than it is for darker or more serious scenes, and the lighting should mirror the pace of the action. Otherwise, the audience will be uncomfortable and sense that something is wrong, though they may not be able to identify the cause specifically. They will have the feeling that a mistake has been made, either in the way the scene was acted or in the lighting, typically the latter.

Keep in mind that the audience perception of the pace of the show relies heavily on the rhythm established by the noticeable changes in the lighting. There is a distinction here between cues that the audience "sees" and cues that have very subtle changes or take place over long periods of time. Sunset cues are a good example of this. The audience notices the effects of the changing light *over time*, without perceiving the actual changes. We usually adjust the speed of these cues — and the moments they are "called" by the Stage Manager — in order to match certain milestones in the lighting change with specific lines or actions by the performers. Here again, the lighting is tied to the performance as it lives on the stage. Remember that the lighting is expressed not only in the levels that are set for each cue, but also in the transitions between cues. The transitions are at least as important as levels in the cues and sometimes even more so.

Cuing the Show

Now that we have explored the significance of the different aspects of cuing, we need to find a place to start the process of entering the numbers into the computer console. It would be wonderful if, on every production, we could sit down at the board with the electrician, have the director nearby, with all the actors on a set that is complete in every detail, start with a blank slate, and meticulously write each cue and set the time for each transition in the show. Well, it might be wonderful in some ways, but everyone would be pretty sick of it in a fairly short period of time. Cuing is one of the most dreadfully boring things in the world for the actors to have to endure. They are asked to stand around onstage and to move only when instructed when they really want and need to be rehearsing. A process like this, where you could take the time to look at the stage from every vantage point and get every level perfect before moving on could take days, even for a short play that doesn't require many cues. Technical rehearsals that are efficiently run and that are planned out so that the actors and crew are called for the least amount of time possible can be exciting and have some fun moments for everyone, but tech days that drag on and drain everyone's energy have had a detrimental affect on more than one opening night.

So, where *do* you begin to cue the show? As with the rest of the design, it begins in your head, but there are guideposts to help you find your way. Most plays and musicals are written with very specific parameters to set the visual context for each scene. Even if the location is only distinguished as "a heath," there is usually some descriptive dialog that helps to further define the lighting. Usually, through the introduction, author's direction, or exposition, the variables of locale, season, weather, and time-of-day are clearly identified. These specifics should not be viewed as restrictions on the design, but as ways to mark both the emotional and physical progress of the play. We noted earlier that the choice of time of day for a particular scene is made to either complement or contrast the emotions of the characters. The *progression* of time throughout the scene should also be noted as playing an important role. A scene that begins at sunset and ends in moonlight has the potential to play host to a wide range of emotions.

Cue Placement

The process of cuing a show begins with identifying *where* the cues are to be placed. This is normally done by marking the script for a play or by marking the script *and* the score for a musical. Music carries powerful emotional motivation for the audience and we have to pay close attention to the ebb and flow of the emotional characteristics of the musical text. The ability to read music, at least to the level of being able to locate the cues, is an important skill. Stage Managers and designers who read music well are a credit to their respective crafts, and they find that they are much more successful when working in the musical genre.

Keep in mind that when we make this first pass through the piece, we are identifying placeholders for changes to the lighting. Cues may be added or subtracted during production meetings and rehearsals, but it is up to the designer to build the framework for the changing lighting environment throughout the production. Once you have identified the basic cues by entering a *Q* next to the appropriate lines or directions in the script, it is a good idea follow along in the script during rehearsals and mark additional locations as they become obvious.

Try to hold off numbering the cues until you are relatively certain that the flow of lighting changes is complete. Also keep in mind that the number of cues in a particular production doesn't matter. Only put in as many lighting changes as the show *needs*. Adding cues to reach a certain numerical goal is counterproductive, eats up additional time in tech rehearsal, and is detrimental to the design. When you do assign numbers to the cues, it should be in continuous succession, without gaps. Most designers start with cue number "one" and continue on from there. For some productions, it may be reasonable to use cue numbers in the 100 range (100, 101, 102, etc.) for Act I, the 200 range for Act II, and so on in order to avoid confusion with sound cues and fly cues being called in a close sequence. Talk this over with the Stage Manager to see what his or her preference is. It is the Stage Manager's responsibility to see that the show runs smoothly every night and his or her insight into the complexities of the production are extremely valuable. Don't forget to include the cues for presets, curtain warmers, house lights, conductor specials, and the like.

Now that you know *where* the cues occur, it's time to determine *what* happens in each one.

Cue Content

If you have the opportunity to go into the theatre and see the cues as you build them on the lighting console, by all means, do so. This technique is especially useful to designers who are developing their skills. This is usually done with an empty stage, so it won't be perfect. Don't take too much time trying to get the level of every channel exactly right because you will make adjustments when the actors take the stage. Establish general intensities, get the sky to look right, and make sure the practicals come on and go off in the right places. Check any special effects and verify that the furniture is on the proper spike mark for the scene in which you are working. Work through the show in sequence, but take breaks at appropriate places to experience brightness adaptation or fatigue in the same way that the audience will.

With the usual time crunch leading up to tech week, it is difficult to find a block of time when no one else needs the stage so that you can sit in the theatre and write the cues on the board. However, it is expected that most of the cues will be recorded into the control console before the first tech, so we are often faced with the task of writing the cues "blind." This is done by sitting down with the script (and the score) and a pad of paper and thinking through the entire show, writing down the intensity levels for each cue and also the fade times for every change. You should find a place where you will not be disturbed while you do this, because you will need to imagine what the lighting looks like through the entire show. If you keep getting interrupted, it's easy to lose track of an important channel that needs to change or to lose a good cue before you finish writing it down. Take breaks when you need to, at the end of an act or after an important sequence, but maintain the continuity and flow of the cuing while you write.

The most efficient way to write a blind cuing session is to only write in the levels that you intend to *change* in each cue. On some lighting consoles, you can elect to use the "tracking" mode, which mimics this method. When you do write the cues in this manner, it is important to write "Change" for each entry until you get to a place where a significant change would prompt you to establish a new look with a different set of levels. At this point, write "New Q" next to the cue number and return to writing in "tracking mode" until another new look is required. Write levels for groups of channels, such as "CH 1-8 ↑ 70%," when you can, using an understandable form of shorthand notation to speed up the process. Using up and down arrows to denote level changes from one cue to the next helps you to keep track of the intent of the cue and makes the changes easier to visualize.

Don't forget to indicate a time, in counts, for each cue change, keeping in mind that different consoles seem to fade at different rates. A three-count or a five-count on one console may not look the same as it does on another, so if possible, you need to become familiar with the count structure of the board that will be used for the show you are working on. If you will not be with the electrician when the cues are loaded into the board, indicate a "default" cue time to be used if you neglect to show a time for a cue or two.

Writing an entire show "blind" may sound intimidating at first, but after the focus is done you will have a good idea of how each channel affects the look of the stage and how to set the levels. It also gets easier with practice. If you are unsure of what the levels should be, it's best to write them a little low and then beef them up selectively during rehearsal. If the whole stage is bright, it's often difficult to see subtle changes in the levels of a few instruments. This is especially true for the director, because he or she doesn't have the advantage of knowing where each instrument is focused. It's easier to see an area get brighter relative to those around it, and it's always better to have the ability to brighten the stage if it is requested. Brightness adaptation due to high intensity levels doesn't leave you any place to go when the director asks for more light and the channels are already at full.

Also, be wary of writing the same cue, or copying a cue, over and over again with the thought of adjusting it to the scene in rehearsal. This creates a trap because of the limited amount of time that you have in rehearsal to rewrite levels for a significant number of channels, and the lighting ends up looking the same in every scene.

Cue Entry

Once you have the cues for the show written down, it's time to enter them into the board. This is done most accurately and efficiently if you can read the levels, times, and cue numbers off your notes to the board operator who "keys in" the instructions to the board. That way you can make adjustments and answer any questions that may come up.

Take the time to review the opening sequence — Preset (Q1), house to half, house out, Warmers out (Q2), Curtain, Lights up (Q3) — to see that everything is operating as expected. Review other sequences and important changes if there is time and make adjustments to the counts in the fade times if you see that they need it. Remember that you are setting the pace for the show through the speed of the changes. Keep in mind, too, that the task at hand is to get all the cues into the board before rehearsal begins. Make adjustments if you can and move on; don't spend a lot of time rewriting the show until you see it with actors onstage.

Bring at least two formatted disks with you and save often, at least after each act. It is disheartening, and creates additional tension and pressure, when you have to repeat entering a long series of complicated cues after someone accidentally kicks the power cord for the board out of the outlet. This happens all the time, so try not to fall victim. Because lighting consoles are so vital to the operation of the show, the next chapter is devoted to the general operating principles of control consoles and some of the pitfalls that experience will help you to avoid.

Chapter Ten
Developments in Lighting Control

Since the onset of the use of diverse types of sources to light the stage, the key to effective design has been the control of those sources. The development of lighting control has followed a progression from various ways of manual control to the computer boards we use today.

The duties of the candle trimmers of old were translated into maintaining various chemical methods of producing light (lime light) and using dowsers for dimming, which then gave way to the use of complicated arrangements of controls called valve tables when gas became a common means of producing light. Each new source produced light more efficiently and with that came an ever-increasing need to have control over the output.

The days of using soot-producing open flames from candles or using chemical reactions with their associated acrid fumes and smoke quickly disappeared as less hazardous methods of lighting were developed. Electric lighting revolutionized the theatre industry, not only in terms of safety but in terms of efficiency and control as well. Developments in conventional lighting, using tungsten filaments and arc lamps continue, while there is increasing excitement over the development of LED (Light Emitting Diode) sources that are suitable for the stage. The trend continues to be toward sources and fixtures that produce more useable light and less heat.

As the sources have become more reliable and sophisticated, so have the means of controlling them. As with the archaic forms of lighting, control of the lights has moved away from manual control of a group of fixtures by an individual to remote control of the entire plot by a single operator. For the designer, this means more precise control and better replication of the intent of the design night after night.

In spite of these advances in lighting sources and the means of controlling them, the way that we approach the translation of the cues from our minds to the stage hasn't really changed much since the times when the first saltwater dimmers were used to vary intensity. For that reason, a brief journey through the development of electric lighting control is in order.

Developments in Manual Control

Electric lights were initially controlled only through switches that allowed current to flow to the lamp filament when "closed" and stopped the flow of current when "open" in the same way that disconnecting a wire would. These were very simple devices, made of copper, with all the conducting or "live" parts exposed. The people who operated the switches were protected from electric shock only by small insulating handles on one end of the switch lever. You had to be careful what you touched and the only people who operated the switching panels were electricians. Liquids, metal, and those unfamiliar with what was safe to touch and what wasn't had to be kept away from the switching "panel" to reduce the risk of serious injury and fire. The panels were located in the wings at stage level where the electricians could see the stage as they ran the show, so people would sometimes inadvertently end up close to the panel. Most actors and other stagehands would stay well clear of the electrical area out of an intense fear of what might happen to them if they got too close. Not everyone understood "the new electricity," but everyone understood that electrocution could cause death quickly, and you may not get a second chance if you touched the wrong thing.

Switching lights on and off at the right moment was an effective, yet not always attractive, way to make the transition from one scene to another. Imaginative electricians could come up with creative ways to sequence certain circuits "on" and others "off" but the change to every circuit was either a "bump" to full or a bump to off. Scientists began looking for ways to control electricity in more subtle ways, not only as it applied to theatre lighting, but mainly for motor speed control and other devices that could benefit from having a range of choices between "on" and "off." There actually was a dimmer that used salt water as a conducting medium to transfer electricity to a metal cone that was lowered into the electrified water. As the cone was lowered and the surface area that came in contact with the energized water increased, more and more power was sent to the light (see figure 10.1). As inefficient, dangerous, cumbersome, messy, and tricky to work with as they were, saltwater dimmers did work.

The principle that the saltwater dimmer worked on was that the less that the cone was in contact with the water, the higher the

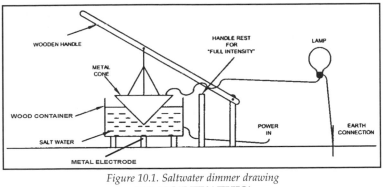

Figure 10.1. Saltwater dimmer drawing
DO NOT TRY THIS!

resistance to the flow of electricity and the dimmer the light would become. This is, in fact, one of the laws that developed from the theory of electricity: the higher the resistance between the source of electricity and the device (in our case a light), the less power will get to the device (the less bright the light will be).

This theoretical knowledge of how electricity behaved led to one of the later developments in dimming technology known as the resistance dimmer. Some examples of this type of dimmer survive and are in regular use today, most often to control house light circuits. The idea was to dim the light by connecting more and more resistive elements between the source and the light. The resistive element was a series of thick, coiled wires similar to that of a toaster or hairdryer. A contact passed along a path that brought more and more of the resistive elements into the circuit, reducing the amount of electricity available to light the light. One of the drawbacks of this type of dimming was that the resistive elements had to dissipate the electrical energy somehow, and just like in a toaster element, they did so in the form of heat.

As is the case with so many mechanical devices, the best way to have the contact travel the greatest distance in the smallest space was to have it travel along the arc of a circle. So, what evolved were resistance dimmer "plates" with the resistive elements embedded in thick ceramic plates (literally), most of which were slightly less than two feet in diameter, with exposed contacts on one side along the outside edge (see figure 10.2). The contact that was connected to the lighting circuit would move along the contacts of the dimmer plate, and as more resistive elements came into play, the light became less bright. Conversely, as fewer resistive coils were used, the light got brighter.

105

*Figure 10.2. Resistance
dimmer sketch*

You can see that as the light output became less and less, the heat output from the dimmers became greater and greater. This got to be a real problem when the design called for large groups of lights to be left off for long periods of time. The dimmer plates would get so hot that they would crack and fail. A way around this problem was to connect the power to the dimmer through one of the switches mentioned in the last section. When a dimmer had to stay "dimmed out" for a long period of time (house lights are a good example), the power to it would simply be shut off. Of course, the problem was remembering to turn the power back on before the next cue to bring those lights up. The switches for this operation were generally located on a section of the panel in front of the dimmer plates through which the insulated handles of each individual dimmer plate would protrude. The electrically conductive parts of the switches would still be exposed, which led to the term *live front switchboard.*

As with switching panels, resistance dimming boards were located in the wings, mainly so the operators could see the stage, but also to keep the cable runs to the lights short. They were often located on the same side of the stage as the fly gallery, which kept the **run crew** closer together and made it easier for the Stage Manager to **call** cues before the days of sophisticated production communication (headset) systems. This meant there was often a lot of hectic activity around the board and more than a few people received a nasty "bite," or worse, from one or more of the exposed live parts.

The resistance boards were not compact devices and required teams of electricians to run a show because of their physical size and the number of handles that needed to be operated for each cue. Many boards were between twelve and twenty feet long, with two rows of control handles and dimmer plates spaced about eight inches to one foot apart (for cooling). Some of the handles could be mechanically interlocked, but there was a limit to how many dimmers a person could control at once due to the force required to move the contacts on several dimmer plates with the control handle. Next to the slot where the handles came through the front of the board, there were marks (usually numbered zero to ten in half steps) so that each dimmer could be raised to a prearranged level that had been set in rehearsal. Each electrician would have a list of dimmers and levels only for the dimmers for which they were responsible in each cue. Sometimes they would have to shift positions like the backfield of a football team during the execution of a cue.

Operators would sit on stools in order to be able to operate dimmers with their hands and feet at the same time. Some of the people who made a living at this were very accurate, both at hitting the correct levels and in making the changes over the correct period of time. Others were not so precise. There was always room for error to creep into the running of the show, no matter how dedicated the operators were. Parts of a cue might be finished sooner than others, and once a cue was "complete," a forgotten adjustment or a setting that was off by a point or so in one direction or the other was left as it was, so as not to chance distracting the audience in order to make a minor adjustment. The cues were often very close from night to night, but not in the precise way that is expected today. Many theatres still show the remnants of a "safety line" that was painted on the stage floor in front of the board to delineate the space where only the electricians would venture with confidence.

Autotransformers

The next major step in dimmer technology was the introduction of the autotransformer style of dimmer. This device was developed specifically for an alternating-current (AC) electrical system as opposed to the resistance dimmer that was developed during a time when direct-current (DC) electrical systems were common. Alternating current was developed as a more efficient way to send electricity over long distances as the power "grids" became larger and larger. Resistance dimmers survived the transition from DC to AC because they could operate on either.

Autotransformers were designed to take advantage of the expanding and collapsing electromagnetic field of the alternating current system. The contact on the dimmer that was connected to the lighting circuit would travel along a wire in which voltage was being "induced" by the electromagnetic field. This was much more efficient than a resistance dimmer because the transformer would only be "tapped" at the voltage required to bring the lamps on the circuit to the desired intensity. Therefore, all power that was available at the dimmer did not have to be dissipated in the form of heat; it simply was not in demand.

Another problem that was eliminated by the introduction of autotransformers was the need for "ghost loads." If a resistance dimmer was rated for 1,800 Watts, the wattage of the lamps connected to it would have to total close to 1,800 Watts or they wouldn't dim out all the way. This phenomenon was referred to as "ghosting," and the way to solve it was to assign "ghost loads" to the dimmer. As a result, there would be lighting fixtures or heating elements in the basement of the theatre that would be connected to a dimmer and never be seen, just to bring the load on the dimmer close to its rated capacity. Autotransformers don't have to have a load assigned to them to match their rating, with the added advantage that they are much smaller than resistance dimmers that have the same power-handling capabilities.

Autotransformer boards were still quite large, some even three times as long as the resistance dimmer boards they replaced, and the control handles were still mechanically connected to the dimmers themselves. They were more efficient and reliable, and the heat dissipation was lower, but the means of executing a cue was exactly the same: a group of electricians would manually move the dimmer handles, each trying to match the number of counts in the cue while attempting to get each dimmer to the correct level. As with resistance dimmer boards, the cues were typically pretty close, but not all the time. Figure 10.3 shows a somewhat unusual arrangement with the control handles on the horizontal surface rather than the vertical surface.

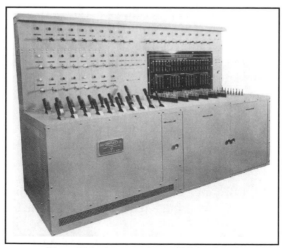

Figure 10.3. Autotransformer lighting board
(Courtesy of Strand Lighting)

The Patch Panel

Another important part of the dimming system that was developed during this era was the patch panel. This is an intermediate connection point between the dimmers and the individual circuits throughout the facility. The patch panel was developed at a time when there were many more circuits in theatres than there was room for dimmers, where each dimmer had the capacity to operate the lighting instruments on several circuits. As a result, a number of circuits would be selectively "ganged" together at the patch panel in a manner that made sense for each new show and plot.

The way this worked was that each dimmer had a number of "appearances" or receptacles at the patch panel, usually on the vertical surface at the back (see figure 10.4). There were typically four or six appearances per dimmer, depending on dimmer capacity, with the number of the dimmer engraved above a row of receptacles. The individual circuits were connected by a flexible cable to a plug that rested on a horizontal surface in front of the dimmer appearances. Each plug had the circuit number engraved in the surface next to it; the number would also be engraved on the back of the plug so that the number could be read off the plug while it was plugged into a dimmer socket.

Figure 10.4. Patch panel sketch
(Courtesy of Strand Lighting)

Even in smaller theatres, the way that the show was patched required careful consideration on the part of the designer so that the dimmer board could be operated efficiently, with the fewest people and in a way that provided the greatest opportunity for the operators to get the cues right every night. Patching also required careful planning and meticulous routing of the plug wires on the part of the Master Electrician, especially for any circuits that were to be "repatched" during the show. The part of the patching arrangement that survives in the computer boards of today is the selective assignment of circuits (dimmers) to a logical sequence of control locations (channels) on the control surface. More on that shortly.

Remote Manual Dimmer Control

Research into finding efficient ways to control alternating current electricity continued. As with the LED technology that is developing today, the problem for theatrical applications was having the capacity to handle higher levels of power and heat than would be required for many other applications. There were a number of developments that led to the next significant breakthrough in theatrical dimming, which would allow the dimmers to be controlled remotely. Some of the experimentation involved technology that was borrowed from successes with high-powered radio transmitting tubes, while other solutions tapped more exotic technologies of the day.

By far, the biggest leap in dimmer technology was made with the development of a solid-state device called the Silicon Controlled Rectifier (SCR), which still has the widest acceptance for this purpose today. The SCR is basically a high-speed switch that can be used to control the amount of power that is delivered to a lighting instrument. SCRs are used in matched pairs to control the positive and negative portions of each alternating current cycle, which in the United States occurs sixty times a second. The electricity that is being controlled is 120 Volts, standard household voltage. Solid-state (transistor-like) rectifiers had been around for a while in the form of "diodes," but they hadn't been used for dimming because they lacked the ability to handle the power levels required. Attempting to use these early rectifiers would have been comparable to connecting a piece of garden hose between two pieces of fire hose, sending water through at full pressure, and expecting the garden hose to regulate the flow of water without the system blowing up. But SCRs were developed to handle the power, and they even have the ability to switch that power on and off at computer-like speeds.

Production SCR dimmers were housed in metal boxes equipped with individual fans to keep the SCRs and the "drive" electronics cool. As always with dimming, the enemy of the components is heat, and this is especially true of solid-state components. The technology has continued to develop to the point where today's SCR dimmers are typically rated at not less than 96 percent efficient, and there are two 2,400 Watt dimmers mounted in a module that is less than half the size of the single 2,400 Watt dimmer boxes that were common for so many years.

The development of remotely controlled dimming impacted theatre operations in three significant ways. First, the dimmers no

110

longer had to be located in the wings for the electricians to see the stage, so they could be located in a room where the fan noise could be isolated. Second, the number of people required to execute the lighting cues for the production was reduced, usually to one or two. Third, the control for the dimmers could be located in the Front-of-House, where the operator could see the entire stage and have a view similar to that of the audience.

The most common method of controlling the dimmers was to use several banks of sliders (potentiometers) to send a control voltage (typically 0–10 Volts) to the "drive" circuitry ("brains") of the dimmer. In this way, while the "scene" or bank of sliders we'll call *A* was being used to control the lights that were lighting the stage, the operator could set up the levels for the next scene (preset) on another bank of sliders, *B*. When it came time to change cues, the operator would use a cross fade control (master potentiometer) to fade out scene *A* and fade in scene *B*, using the count times set by the designer. Now that the sliders in scene *B* were active and the sliders in scene *A* were off line, scene *A* could be reset for the next cue. This process would be repeated over and over many times during the show. Many controllers were set up this way, hence the common use of the term *two-scene preset.*

There were some controllers that could be configured with five or more presets, but the consoles would have to split into two or more pieces, they took at least two people to operate, and they were less reliable because of all the interconnections between the console sections and the dimmers. The boards were still manually controlled and the operators would have to set, check, and recheck the level settings for each cue according to the cue sheets that were finalized during the rehearsal process. The cue sheets were often a page or more each because they couldn't be written in shorthand "tracking mode." The level for each slider had to be noted for each cue in order to avoid the confusion that would otherwise ensue. The control of the dimmers was done from a location remote from the dimmers, but it was still manual control. Even as this type of controller became more sophisticated and SCR dimming continued to develop, the patch panel survived as a vital intermediate connection point between the dimmers and the lighting circuits.

Remote Computer-Based Control

The next inevitable leap in dimmer control consoles came with the introduction of computer hardware coupled with specialized software programs to set, record, and recall all the information needed to control the dimmers for the entire show. It is important to note that this is where we depart from manual control of setting the levels and the timing of the lighting changes. Yes, the operator is called upon to press the "Go" button on a computer console when the cue is called by the Stage Manager, but all the information about level settings, patching, cue timing, and special lighting effects is stored in the console and (hopefully) on several disks. The operator can keep track of the level changes and cue timing in real time on a monitor during the show, but there is rarely the need for intervention on the part of the operator except in case of an emergency.

Other information that is entered into the console fades from importance as the cues are finalized and the final look of the show is recorded. You do have the option of viewing individual "cue sheets" on the console monitor if you wish, and you can even print out all the cues for a show, but this is rarely done on a regular basis unless there is a reason to document every level and change in hard-copy format. One reason for this is that such a document just isn't viewed as being a crucial backup in most applications. Furthermore, the number of cues seems to have grown exponentially with the common use of computer consoles, to the point where printing the cue sheets for a modest show could tie up the lighting console and a printer for at least a half hour. Typically, there are sufficient means to back up all the information for a show on stable electronic media, so there isn't a need to generate and store all that extra paperwork. This is not to say that entering, storing, and "playing back" all of the lighting information for a show on a computer-based system is devoid of difficulties, but we can become aware of the potential problems and reduce the risk of information loss or corruption by anticipating them.

112

Chapter Eleven
Computer Consoles

Basics of the Console

Rule #1: Save Often

As with any computer-driven activity, the first rule of protecting your work is to save often. On many computers, there is an auto save feature that can help with this, but this is not typical of most of the consoles that are specifically designed for lighting control. The console is frequently being instructed by the operator to record cues, but the memory location to which they are saved is designed to be successively overwritten and does not reside in what would be considered non-volatile memory.

The only way to be sure that the information in the board has been saved to a more stable location is to save it to a disk using the drive provided for this in the console. Different manufacturers may handle this in different ways, but the drive is typically meant to take 3-1/2" floppy disks. The consoles have a function to format disks, but it is wise to bring a disk that is preformatted, because the action of formatting a new disk has sometimes been known to corrupt or erase all the show information (in certain boards on certain days) before the show can be recorded. This can be particularly disastrous if you wait until after final dress rehearsal to record the show to disk for the first time.

Saving to a disk won't guarantee that you will never have a problem, but it takes care of 90 percent of the electronic glitches and human errors that can creep into the process of cuing and running a show on a computer-based system. Let's start with a review of how these systems work, and then we can move on to the process of building a show in the board.

The Role of the Computer-Based Lighting Console

The concept of remotely controlled dimmers is one that escapes many theatre people, even some seasoned veterans. The idea that a computer console plugs into a standard receptacle and yet powers all the lights in the theatre is a common misconception. In reality, the console is running the operating system for the software, providing an interface for the operator through specialized keys and functions and sending control signals to the dimmers that are located in a metal cabinet, called a dimmer rack, in a conditioned room somewhere else in the building.

The actual dimmer racks are seldom seen by most of the building staff, and it is, unfortunately, not unusual for lighting board operators in some situations to have no idea where the dimmer racks are or not have access to the room in which they are housed. Access to dimmer rooms is typically limited because they are designated electrical rooms with lots of power. Even smaller systems with one or two dimmer racks are fed with hundreds of **amps** of electrical power through wires that have roughly the same diameter as a quarter. This is where the power to run the lights comes from, not the console.

Remember, the lighting computer console is simply a sophisticated way of managing what the dimmers are doing from moment to moment. All the signaling that is required between the console and the dimmers is carried over a few wires about the size of a .05mm mechanical pencil lead. In the days of the slider-type boards, a large bundle of small cables would carry analog signals, typically in the 0–10 Volt range, to the dimmer location. A digitally multiplexed signaling system known as DMX is in widespread use in the lighting industry today but even that is being overshadowed by control protocols that use the popular and computer-friendly CAT(egory) 5 style of network communications wiring. Whatever the style of control or the type of signaling system, the power to run the lights is derived from and controlled by the dimmers (see figure 11.1).

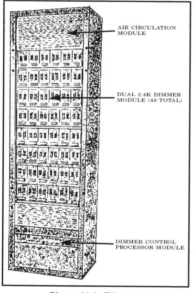

Figure 11.1. Dimmer rack sketch

AIR CIRCULATION MODULE

DUAL 2.4K DIMMER MODULE (48 TOTAL)

DIMMER CONTROL PROCESSOR MODULE

Dimmer racks are often outfitted with two fans to draw cooling air across the plug-in dimmer modules and the resident control electronics. Each module usually contains two 2,400 Watt dimmers, and full size racks are generally configured to hold forty-eight of these modules. That means that a fully loaded, full size dimmer rack will hold ninety-six dimmers rated at 2,400 Watts each. This is enough dimming capacity to safely operate 400 of today's most popular fixtures, rated at 575 Watts each. This may seem excessive until we look at how the systems are designed and used, which we will do by looking at how lighting systems have evolved.

The Development of Lighting Systems

Stage electricians recognized early on that they needed a better way to get power to the lighting instruments than by running miles of heavy-duty extension cables from the dimmers to the lights. This was a time-consuming and difficult task because most theatres of the time were not built to accommodate the need to run electric wires through them. It wasn't long before the extension cables were numbered on each end and left in place in order to save the time and effort required to remove and replace them for each new show. The electricians knew where the wires had to go, but the number of circuits that would be needed at each location varied from show to show. The crew would often have to spend time supplementing the cables that were left in place with additional cables. There were always more circuits than dimmers because the fixtures on a few circuits would be grouped together and connected to a single dimmer.

The connection of selected circuits to a specific dimmer is what led to the development of the patch panel. With the patch panel, systems could be designed with numerous outlets on the electrics — numbered and spaced for convenience — at all the locations where they would be needed. Outlet spacing varied depending on the location of the electric, but the idea was to eliminate the use of long extension cables and limit the need for short cables by placing the outlets close enough to the instruments that they could be plugged directly into the system without **jumpers.** Modern theatres have outlets spaced an average of eighteen inches apart on every electric batten, which keeps the need for extension cables to a minimum.

Modern Lighting System Design

As solid-state dimmer technology has advanced, the dimmers have gotten smaller, more efficient, and less expensive. Along with the development of computer lighting boards, this technology has led to a different way of thinking about how to best design performance lighting systems. The current basis of design for all but the most unique systems is known as the dimmer-per circuit

115

system. This means that every outlet in the performance lighting system is wired to its own dimmer. If there are 288 outlets in a theatre, there are 288 dimmers as well.

As with closely spacing the outlets, this may seem excessive, but it has a number of distinct advantages. The first is, it eliminates the need for the patch panel. Every outlet (circuit) is permanently connected to a dimmer so when that dimmer receives an instruction from the console to come on at a certain level, the resulting voltage is sent to that outlet. Gone are the days of the twisted mass of cables plugged into sockets in the patch panel, the hassle of maintaining thousands of feet of extension cables, and the troubleshooting nightmares that came along with using them. Extension cables and jumpers are still a necessity, but cable inventories are a quarter to a third of what they were prior to the dimmer-per-circuit scheme of wiring. "Patching" is still required, but it is done in the console, electronically.

ASSIGNING CHANNELS

What we call patching now is the act of assigning the dimmers and their associated circuits to channels in order to create a logical sequence of control groupings for each show. Let's say, for example, that we want the fixture plugged into circuit 1 and the fixture plugged into circuit 157 to always come up together at the same intensity. We could assign dimmer 1 and dimmer 157 to channel 1, or any channel number, using the patch function on the console. Now, if we want to have the ability to vary the intensity of the two instruments independently, we could assign one dimmer to channel 1 and the other to channel 2, or whatever channels we wanted. The idea is to group fixtures by color, function, location, and purpose in order to make it easier to keep track of the Light Plot in your head as well as to make inputting and adjusting the cues faster, easier, and more likely to be accurate.

Channel assignments usually start with the front light Front-of-House (FOH) positions, with the downstage right warm or cool assigned to channel 1. In this way, as the channel numbers progress across the stage from stage right to stage left, they "read" correctly in ascending order from left to right for the board operator. Each show will have different demands, and the right combination of channel assignments is one that will result in efficient operations, especially during rehearsal.

Saving Information

After the lights are hung, patching is the first action involving the control console to store information about the show. It is also an excellent time to start recording back-up disks to save the patch information. Many a patch has had to be entered into the board for a second (or third) time because someone came into the theatre and, seeing no cues in the console, loaded the cues from the last show or reverted the patch to "1-to-1" in order to be able to get some lights on quickly. Any information about your show that is in the console is valuable and worth saving. You may not be around when the patch is done, so make sure that the Master Electrician has disks and instructions to record the patch when it is done.

Relying on the disk that resides in the board to record your show is probably not the best idea. There is a good chance that disk has been overwritten hundreds of times, and it may have bits of information from several shows on it. It might record a new show just fine, but you may have trouble retrieving the recorded information at a crucial moment. The label on that disk is probably from three or four shows back at least, so even if your show was recorded, no one would know where to find it without loading the disk into the board to see what was on it. And what if it's not the current show? Ooops!

Try not to be too obsessed with having backups, but do record at least two disks besides the one that is in the board, and keep at least one disk off site. Make sure that the people who might need access to the off-site disk know how to get it if they need it. Trying to write cues on the fly and run a show "manually" on submasters on opening night because no one knew where the extra backup disk was is no fun for the operator, the Stage Manager, the cast, or the crew. Meanwhile you get to sit there and cringe in your seat because you are not seeing the cues that you wrote (and most of them looked *real* nice), and you get tagged with a lousy review to boot. Don't be a victim of the technology; use it wisely and *save often*.

Console Operations

What Keys Do What?

Each dimming system manufacturer sets up the console interface in a unique way and has a proprietary software operating system to go along with it. The best guide to the operation of a specific console is the operating manual provided by the manufacturer. These are written with varying degrees of usefulness for the end user, and some of your success with console programming will depend on your experience with a number of different consoles. Specific keystrokes will vary from board to board, but the operations themselves are similar. Most consoles are set up to be used with an associated video screen so the operator has a visual reference to perform certain operations or to track the progress of the cuing sequence during the show. We'll now take a look at the operations performed with the console and some of the ways those operations can be achieved.

SOFT PATCHING

As noted earlier, the first operation that involves inputting and saving information in the console is patching. Patching is considered an off-line function and can be accessed through the Set Up menu or through one of the "soft keys" located near the top of the keypad area.

On most boards, once you are in patch mode, all you can do is patch. What we are doing when we patch is assigning the dimmers that operate specific lighting instruments to the channel numbers we have chosen to control them. Remember that we are assigning dimmers to channels because each dimmer is wired to a single outlet somewhere in the theatre and we want to organize the control of the outlets into logical groups and sequences for each production. In this way, soft patching has the same purpose as the patch panels of years past. That is, to arrange the control of various groupings of lights into a sequence that makes sense for *this* production. Another way to look at it is that we are customizing the control board to make it easier to program and run a particular show.

It is usually the Master Electrician who sits at the console with the Plot and matches the channel numbers that you have placed with the instruments to the circuit (dimmer) numbers that the electricians — who hung and plugged in the instruments —have written in. One keystroke sequence that might be used to achieve this reads something like this: [DIMMER] [1] [@] [1] [ENTER]. What we have done is to assign dimmer 1 to channel 1 by pressing the DIMMER button, followed by the number "1" button and the "@" button, followed by another stroke of the "1" key. Notice that the latter part of the operation did not require the operator the press the CHANNEL button as the board is in patch mode and automatically brings up the "Channel" prompt. When the number "1" button is pressed again, the channel is selected. We then press ENTER to complete the transaction.

Not all consoles would be patched in exactly this way. Some boards do require a stroke of the "Channel" key to make the channel assignment, and some consoles reverse the selection sequence. Whatever the sequence is, it is repeated until all the dimmers that will be utilized in the show have been assigned to control channels. It is possible to assign more than one dimmer to a channel. In fact, all of the dimmers could be assigned to a single channel, but this would place severe limitations on the choices for varying the lighting during the show.

One of the options available in patch mode on most consoles is the 1-to-1 function. It acts like a reset button for the patch settings by assigning each dimmer to a channel with the same number. When the 1-to-1 function is used, dimmer 1 is assigned to channel 1, dimmer 2 is assigned to channel 2, and so on for every dimmer in the system. This is a way to have quick control over all the dimmers without having to assign channel numbers to each individually.

The 1-to-1 function differs from the Clear Patch function in that the instruction to "clear the patch" unassigns all of the dimmers from channels. Remember that a dimmer must be assigned to a channel in order to use the channel commands on the board. Dimmers that are not assigned to a channel can only be brought up if the DIMMER button is pressed first. If the patch has been cleared and the console is not in dimmer mode, none of the lights will come on. Keep in mind that most consoles default to channel mode when they boot up so that the "Stage" screen is active and the console is configured to execute show commands entered by the board operator.

The channel commands are used to write cues and to perform most of the operations that pertain to recording and "playing back" the show. The 1-to-1 function allows the operator to match each dimmer to a channel having the same number and be able to control the lighting when the console has not been programmed for a specific show. Also keep in mind that if a dimmer is not *unassigned* from or "taken out of" the patch during the patching operation, it remains patched to its like-numbered channel. Clearing the patch eliminates all channel assignments so that you can start with a clean slate when you begin to patch the show. The 1-to-1 and Clear Patch functions are useful shortcuts, but they can have disastrous effects if used at the wrong time. It only takes a split second to wipe out what could be an hour or so of work if either of these functions is executed after the patch for a show is done but not saved to disk.

The patch is completed at the time when the lights are hung, and the console may sit for a couple of days between the day the lights are hung and when the show is focused. It may also sit for a time between focus and the time when the cues are entered. These are the times that it is most likely for the patch to be lost, because the console will probably default to the "Stage" screen when it is turned on, and the fact that something is patched differently will not be displayed on this screen. Someone who has been asked to "turn some lights on" on the stage will find that nothing looks the way it did the last time they did this, and they may attempt to revert to another patch in order to get the lights to look right. As long as you have your disk with you, it takes but a few seconds to reload the patch and any other information that you may have entered that is specific to your show. If not, the entire patch has to be keyed in again.

Once the patch is done, there should be no need to return to this function for the rest of the show, unless there is a change. You may have to revisit patch mode if you hang a new light or if a certain channel "falls out" of the patch for some reason, but this function only becomes important again if something happens with the channel assignments. The patching information resides in the "show specific" portion of the memory, it is active when the board is on, and it is recorded each time you record the show to disk. Once the patch is complete and verified, it's time to record a disk (or two) and move on to entering the cues.

CUE INPUT

Keying in cue information differs from patching in a number of significant ways. First, the console is in stage or "live" mode, which usually means that you can see the effects of the changes that are made to the channel levels both on the stage and on the console monitor screen. Second, the strings of information that are entered are typically longer, increasing the level of concentration required. Third, the element of timing has to be brought into the equation.

Again, when you enter the cues, remember to include all of the pre-show looks, a glow onstage just before the curtain (if the curtain is used) so the actors can take their places in safety, and intermission and post-show lighting changes. If you note them in your script, you can avoid the common pitfall of calling the first look after the curtain goes up "Q1," and then having to renumber or find a clever work-around to avoid having to renumber all the cues in the show. Renumbering cues on a lighting board is very different and much more cumbersome than other types of renumbering functions that we perform using other computer-based systems. But before we get into that, let's look at entering the cues in the first place.

Again, each board may require a different set of keystrokes, but entering a cue might go something like this (note that the board is in stage mode and will recognize number keystrokes as channels): [1–8 @ 5] [ENTER] [9–16 @ 3] [ENTER] [43–45 @ 15] [ENTER] [RECORD Q] [1] [TIME] [5] [ENTER]. Imagine that what we have done is to bring up a warm glow on the front curtain by bringing up channels one through eight to 50 percent and channels nine through sixteen to a level of 30 percent. Backstage, we are providing a slight glow for the crew by bringing up the backlights on channels forty-three to forty-five to a level of 15 percent. We have chosen to call this "Cue One" and when the "Go" button is pressed, it will fade up in five counts.

To clarify the last sentence, most consoles boot up to (an imaginary) "Cue Zero," and the time base that a console uses to fade in and out isn't always measured in seconds. It may sound odd, but certain brands of lighting consoles seem to be decidedly slower or faster than others when they execute a fade. It helps to become familiar with a number of different brands of consoles and to take note of any timing differences that you may notice.

Back to our "Cue One," if everything remains static until the start of the show, this cue will typically be "up" for a half hour or more, so try to keep the levels fairly low and avoid using instruments that have blue color media in them because the heat buildup over time is considerable. Obviously, if the curtain is open and you need blues in the show "preset" to paint the stage while the audience is entering, so be it. Just be prepared to change the color in those units often in order to maintain the look.

In our next lighting action, we will probably want to take the stage to black just before the play starts. Having recorded the preset as "Q1," we then would bring all the levels to zero [1–45 @ 0] [ENTER] and record a fade to black in seven counts [RECORD Q] [2] [TIME] [7] [ENTER]. After the curtain has been drawn or the actors have taken the stage in darkness, we are ready to bring up the lights on the first scene. Before we do that, let's look a little more closely at the interaction with the console, keeping in mind that the exact sequence of keystrokes and the command names may vary across the range of products available.

Maneuvering the Console:
Avoiding Common Pitfalls

RECORDING A DARK CUE

If you are in a cue and you wish to take the stage to black, one of the most common ways to do this is to press [1–(maximum number of channels for this console) @ 0] [ENTER], making sure that you or the board operator call out "stage going black" before the ENTER key is hit. This warns anyone on the stage or in the wings that the lights are going out and that they should freeze for a few seconds while the cue is being recorded. Once a dark cue has been recorded, back up into the last cue or bring up a few channels that you have assigned to a submaster at a glow just for this purpose. This will allow people to move about the stage safely, and if you have gone to the previous cue, it will allow you to see the cue sequence through the transition from light to dark to light after the next cue has been recorded.

A fade to black, a blackout, or a bumpout all end with the same result — a dark stage — the only thing that's different is the time that it takes to achieve darkness. A **blackout** is a fade to black that is written with a fade time of zero. Some directors and designers use the terms blackout and bumpout interchangeably; others feel that there is a distinction between the two. A **bumpout** may be considered to be slightly longer than a blackout, but probably no longer than a count of .5, one half of a full count. The difference may sound miniscule, but the effect is noticeable depending on how many instruments are up at the time, the types of lamps they use, and the function of the instruments.

Color is another factor in *perceived* fade time. Using a sky drop, fade each of the primary colors from full to zero and from zero to full in the same short fade time and see which ones seem to fade in and fade out the fastest. A fade to black, a fade all, or an MFO (master fade out) can vary greatly in duration, but all would generally be thought of as being one count or longer. The point is to work out a code that you and the director agree on, being sure you each understand what the terms mean, and stick to it. Again, we are trying to describe visual phenomenon verbally, and we need to strive for clarity and avoid confusion in our verbal communications. One's sense of fade time (in or out) is affected by many factors, so it is important to remain open to interpretations regarding speed, while keeping in mind that the movement of the lights plays an important role in setting the pace of the production.

COMMUNICATING WITH THE BOARD OPERATOR

It is also vital that you develop a good routine for verbal communication with the board operator. A few erroneous keystrokes or a misinterpreted instruction can raise tension levels and wreak havoc with the production schedule. Both you and the "board **op**" have a responsibility to concentrate and stay focused as you work together to translate the flow of the lighting cues into the machine language of the console. This point may seem obvious, but it is raised here because many of the operations that are performed on the lighting console in the heat of rehearsal are automatically (and incessantly) interrupted by the screen prompt "ARE YOU SURE?" This prompt appears whenever the RECORD or DELETE key has been struck and you are completing the action using the ENTER key. The sequence could be something like [RECORD Q] [9] [TIME] [5] [ENTER] —ARE YOU SURE? — [ENTER].

The prompt appears each time a cue is recorded and with good reason. It builds in a pause so that you can check what is on the screen before it is saved to the internal memory of the console. The problem is that the prompt appears so routinely that many board operators develop a habit of automatically hitting the ENTER key twice for every operation, without really checking the screen. This is a commonly accepted practice that goes unnoticed until a cue is inadvertently wiped out and valuable time is lost trying to rebuild it.

It is best if the board can be brought into the house and you can sit at a "tech table" with the console and the operator. This way you can communicate with each other directly and you can check each other's work as you go through the process. Be sure that the monitor for the board is angled away from you so that it is not adding an element of brightness adaptation to your perception of the cues, but place it in a location where you have a view of the information displayed on it.

This brings up another point regarding why the designer shouldn't operate the lighting board during rehearsals. Not only is the focus of each job very different, but as the board operator your eyes also have to constantly adjust from looking at the screen to looking at the stage. It takes time to make the transition (to adapt to a different brightness level) and as a result, you lose track of the flow of the lighting on the stage.

Whether you are able to sit with the board operator during rehearsal or not, take some time to discuss the procedures and protocols for cuing the show before rehearsal starts. You can emphasize that you would like to take advantage of the pauses that are built into the process and the program in the "ARE YOU SURE?" prompt by making sure that the operator is at least prepared to hesitate before hitting the ENTER key for the second time. After you have a cue set, you might call it by the wrong number or the operator may mis-key the information into the console, but whatever the reason for the mistake, time is lost (along with a good cue) and tension is heightened. When this happens, and it will from time to time, it's not an occasion to freak out, stop rehearsal, and storm out of the theatre. You may have to wait until after rehearsal to rebuild the cue, sometimes with better results. What is more important at the moment is to check the status of where the console is in the cue sequence so that you don't continue to overwrite or mis-number any of the cues that follow. The loss of a cue, and the work that went into building it, is upsetting, but the object is to carry on and not to compound the problem by allowing your thought process to be clouded with anger.

Saving a Show

Some of the more global utilities of lighting consoles can be even more detrimental to the preservation of cues and other important information, so it is wise to approach these functions with discretion. It always helps to have a *current* backup disk in case of a mishap, but attempting to save to a disk is, in itself, an operation that must be done in a precise manner. Saving a show to a location other than the memory resident in the lighting console is a function that, like patching, is considered an off-line operation. You typically enter this mode through the Set Up menu or one of the "soft keys," and the other functions of the console are locked out while the operation is being performed, usually for a minute or less. Once you have entered the save mode, you usually have two choices: 1) "RECORD SHOW TO DISK," or 2) "RECORD SHOW FROM DISK." Some consoles will default to option one; others may not.

It may sound unusual, but entire shows have been lost in the execution of this single operation and this is where it becomes important to have a "clean" disk in the board when you want to record your show. If the "resident disk" is in the console and it has last week's (or last year's) show on it and you or the board operator accidentally select option two and hit the ENTER key twice, all of the information about the show you are working on, including every cue and the patch, will be replaced with the information that is on the disk. There is usually no way to retrieve the current show information from the volatile memory in the console because it has been overwritten. On the other hand, if you insert a clean, formatted disk in the drive and try to perform the same operation, most consoles will come back with an error message that reads something like "SHOW NOT FOUND," and a disaster has been averted.

KEEPING DISKS FOR THE SHOW

Once the show is in rehearsal, you will want to have several disks to use exclusively for that show. One disk should remain in the console. This can be the resident disk as long as information from past performances has been deleted and it can be confirmed as being deleted. The board operator should have a disk that can be stored on- or off-site, but away from the console so that the information on the disk cannot be erased or corrupted. The designer should have a disk to keep with him or her through rehearsal and the run of the show.

As the designer, you may want to have two disks that you alternate recording during the rehearsal process. In this way, if something really out of the ordinary happens and the other current disks end up with some "bad" information on them, you can at least revert to the cues from the night before instead of starting from scratch. You have to keep track of which disk is the current one and which is "one night back" and keep them in your possession. Do not be foolish enough to ever leave a disk around with anything but the most current information on it. It's also a good idea for the Stage Manager to have a disk that can be kept with the cue-calling script for the show. That way, there is always a disk on-site when the show is about to run and it is easily located.

Unless you are in a repertory or academic situation, many shows are rehearsed and run without ever having to use any of the disks to load the cues into the active memory of the console. Recovering from extended power outages overnight, power glitches during rehearsal (such as the cord for the board being kicked out of the socket when the board is at the tech table), and a myriad of other computer maladies can be a long and stressful process, or it can be as simple as entering the save mode and selecting "2) RECORD SHOW FROM DISK" [ENTER] — "ARE YOU SURE?" — [ENTER]. It takes a little time to record a few disks each night, but it's well worth the effort. Now that we have touched on some of the more common pitfalls that may be encountered when using computer-based lighting consoles, we can get back to writing the cues.

Imparting the "Feel" of the Show to the Console

The Conversion Process

The process of representing lighting that evokes the locale, weather, season, time of day, and emotional context of the events taking place on the stage through the number sequences and fade times that are recorded onto a computer is analogous to the process of converting and mixing sound through a sound system. In the audio field, engineers sometimes talk about analog-to-digital-to-analog (A-D-A) signal conversions in certain types of sound systems. The process is that of taking the analog electrical signals from, let's say, a microphone, converting those signals into digital information to be sent to the mixing console for processing, and then converting the information back into analog signals to be sent to the speakers. It is the accurate representation of the analog information in a digital format that was the stumbling block to the success of this type of conversion for many years. Once the information is accurately represented in digital form, it can be manipulated easily and quickly to suit a particular application. The analogy to the computer-based lighting console is that we take the cues that we imagine in our mind (analog), convert them to numbers and sequences in the console (digital), and then see them expressed in light on the stage (analog). Just as in the audio world, it is the accurate translation of the analog information into the digital format that determines the success of the procedure.

This conversion process is where the artistic ability and skill of the designer and the board operator come together to create the look of the show. The consoles are capable of vast numbers of operations in a short period of time and can manipulate data in multiple ways to achieve the same goal. As with their digital audio counterparts, computer-based lighting consoles are sometimes seen as unable to replicate the same "feeling" that you can achieve by manually executing the cues. In reality you can replicate emotion, and unlike digital audio, the success of doing so is not dependent on high sampling rates and error checking, but on the skill that you apply in instructing the console to control the lighting in ways that achieve the desired result.

It is important to note here that it is not the intensity settings in the cues that draw the most concern, but rather it is the *transitions between the cues* where the attention is usually focused. Once the levels have been set for a cue, it doesn't make any difference what type of dimming system is used to hold the levels at their assigned values. What does make a difference is how the changes in intensity are executed in order to achieve the intended effect.

In the days of non-remote style manual boards, teams of electricians would try to synchronize as a unit, but they would also watch the lighting change on the stage and make adjustments in timing to get the "feel" of the changes to match the intent, as they understood it. The human element also comes into play when changes are made with remotely controlled manual boards. The operator may take a cue slightly faster or slower on a particular night, or a cue might be written so that certain dimmers lag behind the others in reaching full intensity. This would require the board operator to adjust the individual sliders for those dimmers after completing a cross fade with the scene fader.

There are two main differences between the changes that are made on a computer-based control console and those produced manually. The first is the sheer number of channel values that are being adjusted. With dimmer-per-circuit systems the changes could involve hundreds of level adjustments in each cue — many more than a person or team of operators could keep track of with any accuracy. Secondly, and more importantly, once the Stage Manager has called the cue and the operator has hit the GO button on the console, the cue runs as recorded with little or no human intervention or input. The crux of the matter is that all of the information needed to achieve the desired effect has to be recorded into the console. This is accomplished using the various timing options that are available when entering cues.

The idea that a cue with "feeling" cannot be imparted to a computer console comes from the difficulty that some designers and operators may have in making that analog-digital-analog type of conversion that is required. The console can only perform those actions that have been programmed into it, so it becomes a question of how to tell the console to do what you want it to do in the language that it "understands." Each console is different, but the timing of many events that take place during a lighting change can be adjusted in several ways. Some adjustments are fairly straightforward and readily achieved; others may take considerable time and experimentation.

Timing Cues

The timing aspects of the cues are critical to the success of the design and merit some examination. One of the most commonly overlooked aspects of cue timing is that consoles will typically default to the same in and out times when executing a cross fade. That is, if a time of "5" is entered when a cue is recorded, the console will automatically fade out the last cue and fade in the new cue in five counts. If we want the previous cue (X) to fade out slowly while the new cue (Y) fades in, we have the option to adjust the default timing by making the "out" time "9" and leaving the "in" time at "5". We are setting how long it takes for each portion of the cross fade to be complete. In this case, the new cue (Y) will be complete four counts before the previous cue (X) has faded to zero. This simple adjustment can have dramatic effects on how the transition looks onstage.

We also have the option of writing multiple-part cues and auto-follow cues in order to blend a number of transitions together. We can build "wait times" into cues and have a number of events running at the same time by starting them sequentially. The possibilities are as limitless as the variety of consoles and the development of the software operating systems. The key is to understand what you want the lights to do and to be able to translate that into commands that can be entered into the console and played back when called for. It takes some time to become familiar with various consoles and get acquainted with the particular means of manipulating each type to achieve the looks and transitions you want. As long as you can break down the progression of events through the transition into segments that can be entered into the board, you can write a cue that mimics the operator input and interpretation of a manual console.

Effects

The most challenging programming on lighting consoles is typically encountered when using the "effects" mode. Effects are complicated sequences of lighting changes that have been anticipated by the software developers or requested by people who use the console. They are an attempt to prewrite the intricate codes to control the lights in a "fill in the blanks" format so that they can be customized to the particular requirements of the show.

Some effects, such as a simple chase, are fairly straightforward, and it is relatively easy to see how adjusting the timing or the intensity affects the outcome. Other effects can be extremely difficult for even an experienced board operator to program successfully. Part of the reason for this may be that in many cases the effects section of the console is so seldom used. The thing to remember is, if you anticipate using effects in a particular show, plan *lots* of extra time to program the board. If you have the opportunity, plan to sit with the board operator during the programming session so that you can see how the effects are built and become familiar with the process. This way, you will know the procedure, you will feel comfortable using effects again, and you will be able to assist another board operator in programming the effects if necessary. Use the operators' manual and experiment with different approaches to achieve the results you desire.

Once you have mastered the means of communicating your intent to the console, your cues can have the look that was once thought to be lost with the gradual phasing out of manual controls. The most recent challenge that has been added to the lighting designer's mastery of communicating design intent to the lighting console is in controlling robotic fixtures and accessories.

Remotely Controlled Accessories

As sophisticated as many lighting consoles are, a majority of the ones that are designed for theatrical use fall short of having the ability to be programmed efficiently when they are using devices such as color scrollers and robotic lighting fixtures. This is a temporary situation as the manufacturers work to develop compatible consoles and software that are able to do both well.

A brief look at the development of remotely controlled accessories for standard lighting instruments and the current proliferation of moving light manufacturers will help us to understand the existing situation as well as what may be on the horizon. These developments represent powerful tools for the lighting designer, but with the introduction of these flexible fixtures comes the need to understand how to best take advantage of their capabilities. Understanding good lighting design is the first and most important step in knowing how to incorporate robotic devices into a Light Plot. Remember that just as the paint brush and the paint do not create the painting, lighting equipment, no matter how complicated or expensive, does not create beautiful lighting. It is the artist or the lighting designer with an idea and the skill to bring it into reality who creates the art.

IMPETUS FOR DEVELOPMENT

The desire to change certain aspects of the lighting beyond that of dimming has been with us for quite some time. To some degree, follow spots have been used to fulfill that need on a limited basis. With a good operator, a follow spot can fade up on a performer anywhere on the stage, follow the performer — making adjustments in size if necessary — change color, reduce intensity using the dowser, trade off to another performer or grow in size to encompass more than one person, and fade out at the end of a segment as the rest of the lights come up. That's a considerable amount of sophisticated control, but as long as the lamp stays lit, the effect is only as good as the operator.

Imagine how unmanageable it would be if all of the fixtures in a plot were follow spots. Even if theatres could be designed in such a way that all the operators could have a comfortable place to stand or sit during the performance and all operators were dedicated to their craft, the resulting lighting would probably be quite chaotic and unpredictable. The repeatability factor would drop to a level beneath even what could be achieved on a resistance dimmer board. The cost would be astronomical and would probably exceed the benefits, and there would have to be an enormous pool of highly skilled operators who weren't working on a show in order to cover illnesses, injuries, and vacations. Calling cues would require several headset channels and, most likely, three or four Stage Managers, and most people, including the lighting designer, would probably not be happy with the results. Nevertheless, the use of follow spots fueled the desire to have control over certain aspects of lighting that were static throughout most of the history of electric lighting in the theatre.

CHANGING COLOR

The quality over which it is generally considered most advantageous to have control (and the easiest to address) is color. Designers who worked with Modern dance companies felt a strong need to have this control because of the variety of looks required for a wide range of stylistic differences that would be presented in a single concert. Because the predominant light for dance comes from the side, designers would often have the color on the booms changed during intermission. This tended to divide the program into distinct segments, though, with a more dark, moody group of performances at the beginning and the more lighthearted dances performed in the second part of the program. That way, the audience would be left in a more upbeat mood when the program was over. The designers and the choreographers wanted to have more freedom to mix the pieces for a more balanced program.

In order to achieve this, the designers and dance captains began to train the dancers to change the color in the side light between numbers. Typically the dancers would have access to three or four instruments on each boom, starting with the shin buster on the bottom at one foot off the deck, and then moving up to the mid and possibly a high-mid. Although they couldn't reach the higher units, this wasn't considered a hindrance. You will recall from our earlier exploration of the dance genre that the color for the highs tends more toward the range that is common for acting-area light in order to light the dancers' faces and illuminate lifts. With three to four booms on each side to cover most stages, the dancers could access over thirty instruments for color changes, which had a significant effect on how the dancers looked in the light.

Control of the side light for dance is usually split between stage left and stage right and assigned from bottom to top. That is, the shins on stage right are controlled together and the shins on stage left are controlled together and they would all share the same color for a particular piece. Once again, these are not the "rules" for dance lighting, but general basic practice. So, if a piece featured a lot of precise foot movement and light-colored footwear, the designer would probably opt for a color in the lows that would emphasize the feet to the strongest degree. This is typical of many dance plots anyway, but we might give a little more thought to it and a little more "punch" to the light in this case. This might also be true if the dancers were low to the floor, but pieces that feature this style of choreography often have a "darker" theme, so a more saturated color in the blue or lavender family might be chosen for the shin busters. If the choreography were to feature "freezes" where the position of the torso was combined with angular arm positions, we might place less emphasis on the feet and go with some lighter colors in the mid on stage right and the high mid on stage left, using the other side for contrast.

The combinations could get quite complicated and the color changes would become part of the dancers' choreography. Dancers in many companies became very skillful at making color changes without affecting the focus of the fixtures or making the booms rock back and forth. Some of them also went on to become excellent lighting designers because of the understanding gained through this experience. Occasionally an injury or some other mishap backstage would cause a change to be missed, bringing back that desire to limit the reliance on a team of people to make changes in the lighting. The color scroller was the solution to the problem, and after being developed for use in touring lighting rigs, it was quickly accepted into the theatre for this purpose.

OPERATING SCROLLERS

The operation of the color scroller is fairly straightforward. A series of color media sections that have been cut to the proper size are taped together at the edges to form a "gel string" with a length of clear media at each end. They are then secured to a roller (see figure 11.2). The center shaft of each roller is then connected to a small motor on each side of the scroller. Through the use of some very accurate measuring circuitry in the scroller that tracks the precise position of the gel string at all times, the lighting console can "learn" a value for the location of each color in the string.

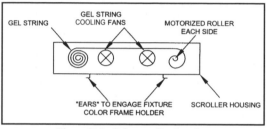

Figure 11.2. Color scroller drawing

Gel strings for a specific function, let's say the mids on the booms or a front wash, are usually built to be identical so that control of them as a group is simplified. Most manufacturers offer a "standard" gel string that is provided with their scrollers unless the purchaser orders a custom string. The communication link between the scroller and the lighting board is set up on the DMX signaling system that is used to control the dimmers. In this way, the control of each scroller can be assigned to a channel on the console and the location of each color can be assigned an "intensity" value for identification.

Once the console "learns" the location of each color, we can label an intensity setting with the color name and number. For example, let's say that the first color in the string for the front wash is a straw and we know that the center of the straw color will be at the center of the instrument lens when we set the intensity of the assigned channel (let's say it's channel 200) to "1." Let's also say that the last color in the string, a deep lavender, is centered on the lens when the channel is set on an intensity level of "10." Most scrollers will accept a gel string of sixteen colors or more, but let's say that the strings we are using have nine colors in them and we have assigned the scrollers to the channels 200 through 206. This means that if we set channels 200 through 206 at an intensity of "1" (10 percent), the straw color will move into position in front of all the fixture lenses. If we select an intensity of "10" (100 percent) for 200 through 206, the deep lavender will be centered in front of the lenses, and if we choose a level of "5," the color in the middle of the string will be brought into place. Choosing an intensity of "1.5" (15 percent) would put half of the first color, the straw, and half of the second color in front of the lens. This is not all that unusual a practice because the gel strings are constructed without gaps and the tape used to build them is transparent.

You can see that if the gel strings were not built to be identical, the intensity setting used to identify each color would be different for each channel, which would complicate entering the commands for changes. Identical gel strings also allow us to gang the control of a group of scrollers to a **"repeater"** and reduce the number of control channels that are used for color control. Each scroller can be assigned a unique "address" so that we can have individual control over it in the same way that we can control individual lighting instrument intensity in a dimmer-per-circuit system. However, if you have 200 individually controlled lights, 100 scrollers, and a 250-channel board, you quickly run into a problem if you want to control all the scrollers individually too. This would be an unusual circumstance, but the chance of running out of channels increases when we start working with devices that require multiple control channels, as we will see shortly.

Other factors that enter into the programming formula are when to change the color and where in the gel string the colors are positioned. Unless we are trying to achieve an effect, colors are typically changed only when the instruments are off, so we have to choose the moments when we change the color carefully and write them into the cues in a precise manner. Scrollers are also capable of changing colors quickly, but they generate more noise when they run at higher speeds, so changing from the straw in the first position to the deep lavender in the last position at an instant when the lights are off can result in a level of scroller noise that is unacceptable during the quiet moments of a production.

Managing the use of color scrollers adds another layer of complexity to the design, along with the requisite charts and tables used to track the values that relate to each color, the channels that operate the scrollers, and the timing and speed of the changes.

MOVING LIGHTS

Once a reliable system to remotely control color was developed and perfected, the desire to affect the other controllable qualities of light from the console became more acute, and robotic fixtures, or moving lights, were created. At first, they were used exclusively on rock 'n' roll tours because their expense and the time it took to program them made their use prohibitive in theatre settings. As more manufacturers have entered the moving light market, the cost of robotic fixtures has come down and more efficient consoles have been developed to program them, making them viable for use in the theatre. It is no longer unusual for small theatre companies and schools to own at least a small complement of robotic fixtures.

The units are capable of various levels of controllable features, which often include intensity, pan, tilt, color, beam size, sharpness, patterns (gobos), gobo rotation, and a host of other effects. Each controllable quality is called an **attribute** and each attribute requires a separate control channel. Many fixtures require twelve to sixteen control channels, but this number can be as high as thirty-two. Trying to incorporate all the flexibility of robotic fixtures into a coherent design can be challenging to say the least, and it is the programming that presents the biggest stumbling block.

PROGRAMMING AND USING MOVING LIGHTS

While moving lights can be programmed on a standard theatrical-style console, it can be a long and arduous process to make even the simplest moves look good. The manufacturers sell proprietary equipment for programming, but each one has it's own style of programming and nomenclature, and a mixture of different robotic fixtures in a plot makes these tedious to use as well. There are a few consoles that have been designed to program a range of robotic equipment, and these are the boards of choice for intense levels of this type of work. As efficient as these consoles are, it takes a considerable amount of skill and experience to become proficient in their use. There is a small group of professionals who travel the world doing nothing but programming tours and permanent installations on these consoles. As the use of robotic fixtures becomes more prevalent in the theatre, manufacturers and professionals are working closely together to produce lighting consoles that are equally well suited to operating robotic and conventional lighting, but we're not there yet.

This information is not presented to discourage the use of robotics, because they will become more and more viable for use in all types of productions as time goes on, but only to make you aware of the challenges they currently present. We have been through a period when the use of moving lights was more of a programming exercise than the result of thoughtful design work. That is to say that the lighting we would see on the stage was predicated more on the fact that the lights are capable of certain spectacular effects than on a connection to the performance itself.

This trend is fading as designers are shifting the emphasis of their lighting designs away from drawing attention to the use of robotics and back to enhancing overall production value. This movement has been augmented by the development of software and consoles that allow the designer to select and program fixtures in a "virtual" environment and then transfer that information directly into the console that will actually run the show.

Moving lights can be an extremely useful tool if they are incorporated into the performance in a way that utilizes their value as a design element and is not driven by a display of effects "because the light can do it." When you begin to encounter moving lights and other remotely controllable accessories for lighting equipment, the key is to allow lots of extra time to become familiar with the technology, what it takes to operate the system, and how the units with which you are working are programmed. In this way you will be best suited to utilize each type of equipment for maximum benefit and in an efficient manner that does not eat up valuable production time when the show goes into rehearsal with the rest of the company.

Chapter Twelve
Tech Week: The Final Frontier

Now that the lights have been hung and focused and we have identified the cue locations and entered the foundation for each cue into the board, we come to the part of the production process where it all comes together, in conjunction with the work of the director, the actors, and the other members of the production team in the final week of rehearsal. It's a busy time for everyone, and an exciting time as well, because this is typically the first time everyone gets to see their work onstage, under lights. The "under lights" aspect of the experience is a crucial one because, up until this point, the performers, costumes, sets, and other production elements have not been viewed in the lighting environment that has been created for the production.

The following chronology is for a theatrical or musical production with a Thursday night opening, on the professional or semi-professional level. The schedule for a production in an academic situation may be considerably different, but the *process* should be very similar. The schedule for the production in our example might go something like the following scenario.

Tech Week Scenario
Saturday
SETTING THE SHOW

This is usually the first time that all of the elements of the completed production are in the same place at the same time. The director, designers, run crew, and cast come together to "set" the show and make adjustments as necessary over the course of a twelve-hour day, with two one-hour scheduled breaks — hence the name "ten-out-of-twelve." The object on this day is to see how the completed visual elements look together under stage light, to verify the proper operation of the various technical systems, set the levels for the sound, and execute every change that happens over the course of the show to find out what is working and what needs to be revised.

When we refer to something that "works" it's not in the purely mechanical sense, but more a determination of appropriateness to the production. If we say that a piece of furniture or a lighting cue doesn't "work," that doesn't mean that something is broken, but rather that it doesn't fit the moment or the play properly. The same term can also be applied to action and direction, or the duration of a scene change.

THE SPEED THROUGH

In order to make these determinations, the cast and crew will often be prompted through a "speed through" by the director and Stage Manager to fulfill the requirement to visit every transition in the show. Usually, the cast will be asked to perform a small bit of business leading up to a cue and then the cue will be executed as it would be in performance. This procedure includes every sound cue, lighting cue, fly cue, and scene change in the show. It may also include working on cues with the conductor for a musical.

THE CHANNEL AND FOCUS CHECK

A channel and focus check is critical before the rehearsal, because a considerable amount of time is devoted to the lighting and it is your chance to set the look of each cue and check the timing of the transitions. This can and must be done quickly, so it is imperative that the blind cues are thoughtfully written and accurately entered. Try to set the final levels for the performance areas and leave other details for another time if you have to, making sure to take good notes so that it is clear what needs to be done when you go back to make the adjustment. Remember, the object is to get through the whole show. Slowing down the process so much that the production staff and the cast and crew have to go into the following day without getting through all the cues steals time from other activities and jams up the schedule.

If you don't have time, don't dwell on details that can be adjusted at another time, but also don't neglect to get the light on the performers correct to the highest degree possible. Things may change before opening night, but once you have set the look, you can make adjustments without compromising the design. If a lighting look has not been established well enough, it is easy to get lost in making adjustments and skew the effect of the cue away from the intent of the design. If there is a series of cues that happen in quick succession, this may also be the last time you have the chance to look at them individually and make adjustments while the cast is asked to wait until the lights are ready. Work with the Stage Manager to keep the process moving and avoid long delays.

Handling Delays

If there is a delay that can't be avoided, use the time wisely to make adjustments that you foresee based on changes that have already been made to a particular look or to the pace of the show. If the console has a bright cue up when a delay is initiated, you may want to have the board operator run the master down a bit to save the color, being sure to leave enough light onstage for the cast and crew to move about safely. Remember not to write cues with the master at reduced intensity and to raise the master back to full when you return to the flow of the production.

If the work lights are up and you can't do anything in "blind" mode on the console, relax, but be ready to go as soon as the delay ends. If the delay is due to a lighting problem, try to arrange it so that the cast can work on other things by providing some light onstage or using work lights. Then work with the electrics crew to resolve the problem quickly so everyone can return to stepping through the sequence of the cues. It seems that no one is immune to delays on this first day, but planning and preparation between you and the crew will keep any tense moments of delays due to lighting problems to a minimum.

Recording Show Disks

Have the board operator record all the show disks and be sure to keep one with you. When this day has ended, you and the crew should be able to go home, get some rest, and come in refreshed the next morning, ready to take care of notes and see the show run in real time.

Sunday

Touch-ups

The actors are usually called for the late morning on this day, but you will probably arrive at the theatre just about the time that the paint on the stage floor is dry enough to walk on. The crew will probably have some work to do dressing cables and organizing the gel inventory while you make some cue adjustments with the board operator. If you notice during channel and focus check that there are any units that need to be touched up, you will most likely want to do that first before anyone else needs the stage. Finish the adjustments onstage first (if the floor is dry enough) so that the ladder or the lift will be out of the way. If you have to wait to touch up some FOH units, you only need to be able to access the focus location and have a few minutes of relative darkness. Having a ladder onstage to focus a light while the actors are being called to their "places" is hazardous and creates tension, so avoid this situation.

THE COSTUME PARADE

The latter part of the morning may be devoted to a "costume parade," where all of the clothing for the production is seen onstage under light for the first time. Even though the clothes may be modeled out of sequence, this is a good opportunity for you to match the cues to the dress for the different scenes. It also allows the costume designer to see each costume in the lighting you have set for the time during the show when it is to be worn. If you have had fruitful conversations with the costume designer, looked at the fabric swatches under light while choosing the colors for the show, and visited the costume shop to see the costumes, there shouldn't be any surprises. If the collaboration between the designers has been good, minor adjustments to the costumes or the lighting should be all that are necessary.

A problem that does turn up on occasion is when people in black costumes appear in blue light. Because of the mixture of dyes that are used to create black material, the costumes may reflect blue light in surprising ways. They will usually appear to be a shade of muddy brown with a hint of burgundy thrown in. It's not too bad if all the material is from the same dye lot and all the costumes are built with the warp or "grain" of the fabric running in the same direction. The real problem comes when a batch of rental costumes contains a mixture of fabrics, or a different dye lot was introduced in a group of stock costumes when some of them were replaced. Both you and the costume designer can avoid an unpleasant surprise if you address this ahead of time.

If there is a delay during the costume parade to make an adjustment, remember to ask the board operator to pull the master down a little to keep the heat off the color media. Make adjustments to cues if you have time (and if they really need it) while the cast is onstage for the costume parade. If not, take notes and look at the cues again during rehearsal.

THE AFTERNOON RUN

The costume parade is often followed by a quick lunch break, the cast gets their call to get into makeup, and the time is set for an early afternoon "go" to run the show. The afternoon run of the show is the first time that everyone sees and participates in the full show in real time, with all the elements fully realized. The show should be complete and ready to go as far as the lighting is concerned.

Remember that, just as it is unfair for the actors to be "on book" late in the rehearsal process, or to skip lines and miss cue lines, it is equally unfair if the lighting is not ready during the tech rehearsal process. Having the actors repeatedly fake their way through missing or incomplete lighting cues makes them feel uncomfortable and throws off the pace of the show. This is especially true for actors who are just developing their craft. It is very disconcerting for any actor to have to go into opening night without knowing what the lights will do or lacking confidence that the cues will happen correctly. The actors are the ones who initially face the embarrassment and bear the burden of covering a mistake. Don't add to their burden by forcing them to work in an unstable or incomplete lighting environment until opening night.

The Stage Manager is in charge of running the show at this point and should call all the cues. This is a time for you to focus on the visual aspects of the show and to be acutely aware of the timing of each event. Try to make an objective assessment of how well the lighting cues and the lighting transitions are tied to the action and the emotion of the show. This is also a time to sit with the board operator and make adjustments if there is time between cues. Remember that when you make adjustments, you have to leave the board operator enough time to go through the [RECORD Q] [#] [ENTER] — ARE YOU SURE? — [ENTER] sequence before moving on to the next cue or the adjustments will be lost. Unless you are changing the timing of the cue, it is usually not necessary to enter the time segment again. If you don't have time to work on a cue while it's up, take clear notes and adjust it later. With the board in the house, you have a good opportunity to check the levels on the monitor and write down very specific adjustments.

HANDLING DELAYS AND BREAKS

If the progress of the show is delayed for some reason other than an emergency, try to hold the mood and help the cast to stay in the moment. If the delay will be longer than a few minutes, use the time in the best way possible, but don't get so involved in doing something that you can't get right back to rehearsal as soon as the cause for the delay has been resolved.

It is also not wise to send the board operator on a break unless there have been specific instructions from the Stage Manager to do so. If you need to leave the theatre briefly, make sure the Stage Manager knows that you are leaving and when to expect you back. Delays make rehearsal tedious for everyone and we want to keep them as short as possible. When rehearsal resumes, do your best to quickly focus your attention back to the lighting and away from any distractions.

When intermission breaks are given during rehearsal, take a break and leave the theatre for a few minutes if you can, or at least try to move away from the tech table for a while. If it's a bright afternoon, come back a little early to give your eyes a chance to adjust. Hopefully, delays will be few and short and the run-through will take only slightly longer than the actual run time of the show.

RECORDING A SHOW DISK

When rehearsal is over, have the board operator record the show disks, one of which you will take with you, while you are waiting for the actors to change and come out for notes.

NOTES

"Getting notes" is a unique way to receive praise and be evaluated, but it is used because it is the most efficient means available. Typically the director is the only one who gives notes during these sessions. Notes from others are related to the rest of the production team through the Stage Manager. Having good things about your work revealed before the cast and crew is something we all enjoy; hearing about mistakes and shortcomings along with everyone else is not. Giving notes is the way that directors communicate adjustments they feel could be made to improve the show.

Most directors are sensitive to the feelings of individuals and are tactful when making an observation about some aspect of the show that could use improvement. Receiving notes should not be regarded as a personal attack by any of the cast, or the design and technical staff. You will also probably find that most directors are also lavish with their praise of individual contributions to the production. Keep in mind that the director will probably have many more notes for the cast because he or she has typically spent more time with the actors and is more comfortable sharing constructive criticism with them than with the crew and the designers, but addressing technical and design adjustments is a job that has to be done. Directors usually have a better understanding of the actor's work as well; that's why they're directors and not designers.

In whatever manner they are presented, getting notes is a time to actually take notes (write them down) and to listen to the observations of someone who has a vision of the production and a global perspective regarding how the various elements are, or are not, working together. Bring the notes that you have taken during rehearsal to refer to, and follow along with the director's comments. You may find it useful to take notes from the director on the same sheet that you use to take your own notes, but if you do this, be sure to distinguish the director's notes in some way. If you skip over one of your notes, you'll probably remember it before it comes up in the next rehearsal, or you can take the note again. If you miss a note from the director, it has to be given again and the director gets the impression that you are not listening well.

That's what a session of "notes" is all about; listening. It is not a time for you to argue, blame someone else, or make excuses. If the director or one of the cast members asks a question or makes a comment that warrants an explanation, try to give a brief, non-confrontational answer. If you really need to have a discussion with the director about a specific cue or the show in general, do so at another time. It may even be preferable to wait until the next day, when you have had some time to reflect on the meaning of the note and you are both more rested. One of the more annoying traits to have to put up with during notes is that of the person who feels compelled to give the director feedback about every note he receives regarding his or her work. It also makes the process longer, which, after a few long days in a row, compounds the annoyance factor. If you are offended by what the director says or how he or she says it, address your concerns in a private discussion at another time.

If you don't get any notes, try to talk to the director for a few minutes as the cast is leaving. You may be able to spark some comments by asking the director what his or her reaction was to a particular cue or transition. The director may tell you that he or she was too busy taking notes about the actors to get anything down about the lights. In this case, use your own notes to stimulate discussion if you can. The director may say that he or she was simply too focused on the action to provide you with reliable feedback about the lighting and you will have to leave it at that. This is not very helpful to the designer, but it usually indicates that there weren't a lot of glaring inconsistencies in the lighting, at least until the show is "on its feet" enough for the director to devote more attention to the lighting. In the meantime, use your notes and general impressions to reflect on the flow and the feeling of the show, and review the concept for the lighting to maintain a point of reference. Try to be objective, don't be too hard or too easy on yourself, and try to look at the show with fresh eyes at the next rehearsal.

ADDITIONAL REHEARSAL

If all goes well, you may see another rehearsal right after a short dinner break. However, if the first rehearsal has gone long and everyone is tired, you may not see another one right away.

Monday

EQUITY DAY OFF

In some professional situations, Monday is known as "Equity Day Off." This is a day when people who are members of Actors Equity, the actors' and Stage Managers' union, are required to be away from the theatre. This rule can be suspended during tech week, depending on a number of factors, including how the actors vote on the question. The rule does not include other members of the production staff, so if there is no rehearsal, it's a good time to make any final adjustments, thoroughly check any equipment that has been giving you trouble, and start to put some polish on some of the cues.

It's also a good day to get another hour or so of sleep and come in a little later. All the departments will have the same idea about starting later in the day, so it is wise to coordinate with the other designers and crew heads to make sure they are not planning on performing some task that will prevent you from completing your work. If you plan on having equipment and personnel onstage or you need to have the stage dark for an extended period, let others know and work out a schedule. Also, be sure to let the electrics crew know well ahead of time if you plan on having a work call on this day. Be sure to perform a channel and focus check before you begin any work.

EVENING REHEARSALS

With all that being said, the cast typically does rehearse the show on Monday, with all the Equity cast members present. If this is the case, it is usually the day when rehearsals are shifted exclusively to the evening hours so that everyone's internal clock begins to adjust to the performance schedule. It is an opportunity for you to make refinements to the cues and make critical adjustments to the timing of the transitions, if necessary.

It is also an opportunity for you to spend more time away from the board and to view the show from different locations in the theatre. If the theatre has a balcony, try to observe as much of the show as possible from the balcony seats, because the way the lighting looks on the floor of the stage will play a much more prominent role for the audience members who have purchased tickets to sit in the balcony. Observe how the show looks from different viewing angles, and take notes or make adjustments if necessary, keeping in mind that the most expensive seats are usually in the center section of the orchestra.

If you are "sitting in a cue" for a while and you can have the board operator adjust levels, remember to do so quickly but accurately and leave time to record the changes without disrupting the flow of the show. After the Stage Manager has called the "warning" for the next cue, it is best to record the changes that have been made and take notes for any additional changes you may want to make.

RECORDING SHOW DISKS AND TAKING NOTES

When rehearsal is over, record all the show disks unless you want to keep one of the previous day's work. Be *positive* that you know which disk this is and *don't* leave it on-site. Pay close attention during notes and make comprehensive notations about the director's observations to add to your list, which should be getting shorter.

Tuesday

REHEARSAL

This is typically a shorter workday, with most of the activity concentrated toward the evening hours and rehearsal. You may want to call the electrics crew before the actors are called, to take care of some final details and work on notes from the night before. Again, be aware of the schedules of the other departments to avoid conflicts in stage time. Be sure to do a channel and focus check, and allow time for the Stage Manager and the run crew to prepare the stage for the evening's rehearsal. Try to take a break before rehearsal and be back in the theatre early so that you are ready for the "Go" or the first downbeat of the music. Let the Stage Manager know where you will be and what time you expect to be back.

Once rehearsal starts, walk the audience chamber and pause to take a seat in different locations to get an overall perspective on how the show will look to the audience. Keep a pad and an inconspicuous light source with you to take notes and jot down observations about any color that may need to be changed before opening night. You can work on finalizing the intermission cues, but the placeholders should already be in the board.

BOWS

This rehearsal is unique in that it is usually the day when "bows" are set. Bows, or the Curtain Call, comprises all that action that takes place after the final scene when the actors return to the stage to receive recognition from the audience and to acknowledge other performing members of the production team, such as the conductor and the orchestra.

As far as the lighting goes, bows usually consist of a single look, with the possible addition of follow spots if they have been used during the rest of the show to highlight certain performers. The cue for bows is usually bright, but it should not be the brightest cue in the show (unless there is a calculated reason to do this). If the cue for bows is brighter than all the others, the audience feels cheated and they wonder why the rest of the show wasn't as bright. Pick a fairly bright cue from the show and make a few minor adjustments for unusual placement of actors if need be. Make sure that you have chosen the cue for bows prior to the time they are to be set, and write it into the board so that the "bows up, bows out" cycle can be repeated a couple of times.

If the curtain is being used, a curtain warmer cue will be required after the final fade to black. If the curtain is not in use, you will need a cue for the post-show preset and you may want to think about why and how it might be different from the pre-show preset. Either type of post-show cue will be accompanied by house lights for the audience to leave and it is best to write the house light cue into the console if possible. As much as the people in the audience might enjoy the production, most of them will want to leave as soon as it is over, and the house lights should be brought up quickly so they are not trying to do this in the dark.

Recording a Disk and Taking Notes

When the final cues are set, have the board operator perform the "record disk" procedure while you collect what you need and find a seat for notes from the director. Everyone should be more comfortable with the process of giving and receiving notes by this time, but don't let that allow you to become complacent about being attentive or writing things down. This is one of the final opportunities for the production team to take the show those last few percentage points toward perfection.

Wednesday

Depending on the company and the circumstances, the activities on the day just prior to opening can fall on opposite ends of the spectrum. If rehearsals have gone particularly well up to this point, the director may declare a day off for everyone. Most of the production staff will avoid the theatre like the plague, but the actors will continue work on their own. The Stage Manager will probably be in to make final preparations for opening night, the set may get some touch up painting, and you may have some notes to go over with the board operator.

OPEN DRESS REHEARSAL

On the other hand, the entire cast and crew may be called for an "open" dress rehearsal where a small audience is invited in, at a reduced cost or no cost, to see the show. This is particularly true in the case of comedies where laughter and audience reaction may affect the timing of the production. The director will usually introduce the show and inform the audience that the rehearsal will only stop if there is a serious problem involving the safety of the cast and crew.

The board will be in the booth and the production will (hopefully) run as if it were opening night. You should "plant" yourself in a location where you can take notes as inconspicuously as possible and only move to a different seat during Act breaks or at intermission. You will have to rely on your script or your memory of the cue placements to take notes about specific cues. You will probably want to position yourself where you can observe the reactions of the audience as well as the stage.

OBSERVING AUDIENCE REACTION

Audience reaction can provide important clues about how well the lighting supports the action onstage. If the audience becomes restless or chatty during a night scene, for example, you may want to consider increasing the light levels slightly for face recognition in that scene, because the restlessness usually indicates that they are having difficulty seeing the actors. The reaction also depends on the content of the scene, and the restless behavior may be just what you were looking for. Also, the reactions of a small audience will vary from those of a large audience because the people are more self-conscious about how their reactions will be perceived by those around them. Remember to gauge your impressions of how the audience reacts with relation to audience size, the composition of the audience members (are they mostly parents or students?), and the type of the material being presented onstage.

Observe the production as an audience member to the greatest extent possible and participate with them in their appreciation of the effort. This may change your outlook in a way that will enable you to perfect a few cues that have been eluding the final adjustment that will take them from good to great.

RECORDING CHANGES AND TAKING THE FINAL NOTES

If you make any changes to the show, the disk recording procedure will be in order. A final round of notes will follow the departure of the audience, and there will be some discussion about how the audience responded to the show. Your perspective on the audience is unique because you have been sitting with them and watching them, so participate in these discussions when the opportunity presents itself.

Opening Night, Photo Call, and Beyond

Opening Night

The anticipation of opening night begins at the very onset of the production process. From the moment that the members of the core production team write down the date or mark it on their calendars, there is a collective effort to arrange schedules and set deadlines for milestones in the process that leads to opening night. On extremely rare occasions, this date will have to be moved (usually due to an unavoidable cast change caused by the death or injury of a principal performer), but once the date is chosen, it is pretty much set in stone. Preparations are made for rehearsal space, the theatre booking is finalized, and the complicated production "machine" is set in motion. Even those who will not be actively engaged in the production until the last few weeks will begin to block out time in order to participate. Much of the impetus for this stems from that adage "the show must go on." The entertainment industry is one of the few that thrives on providing for patrons on holidays and "always being there" even in the face of adversity.

ARRANGING TO WATCH THE SHOW

While we are caught up in preparing the show, we sometimes forget that we need to make arrangements to see the show on opening night. Some companies have agreements with the venue and take care of this completely. There are set numbers of "comps" for the various members of the production team and all the arrangements are seen to. On the other hand, you may go to the box office on the afternoon of opening night only to be told that you can't have a good seat, or any seat, because the performance is sold out. This can be most disappointing, as your attendance is required on opening night and you are still actually working on the show during that first performance. In another case, you may find yourself buying expensive tickets to the opening of your own show. These scenarios can happen at all levels of production because the box office is a separate entity from the production company.

You can avoid this kind of mishap and the frustration that goes along with it by making arrangements directly with the box office. You will want to do this long before the show moves into the venue, and if there is any doubt about how the tickets are being handled, take care of it personally. Once you have made these arrangements, you can look forward to a rewarding and enjoyable night at the theatre.

Before and During the Show

The Stage Manager should be taking care of channel and focus check, but you may want to arrive a little early and discretely check in backstage to see if there are any questions for you.

Planning to bring someone with you to the opening will enhance your experience as an audience member, but be sure to resist the temptation to talk him or her through the entire show as it is happening.

Your notes about the lighting should be limited enough at this point that you can give them from memory and not have to write them down. If you do bring a small pad with you, try not to write notes during the show. If necessary, jot things down during intermission or the end of the show instead. It is not acceptable to use a flashlight or book light to illuminate the pad so that you can write notes while sitting in the audience.

After the Show

The director will generally have a brief note session with the actors immediately following the show, which is a good time for you to give your notes to the crew. The Stage Manager may attend notes with the actors so you may have to wait to give notes about cue calls.

After the notes session there may be a brief get-together with some of the theatre patrons before you leave the theatre, and then it's off to the cast party. During the cast party, you may have some business to go over with the director and the Stage Manager and possibly some of the crew, but then try to take time to appreciate the production as a whole and the contributions that everyone has made. Listen to the perspectives of the actors and answer questions they may have about the choices that were made for the lighting. Try to take away general impressions from the comments that are made without getting caught up in the details. This is the beginning of the reflective process that is essential to the growth of every designer. Graciously accept praise as well as advice on how to make improvements.

Photo Call

A photo call will generally be scheduled after a performance during the run of the show and it is usually approached in one of two ways. Some directors will want a record of the performance exactly as the audience saw it. Others will want to enhance the look of each shot for better photographic quality. Either way, you will want to be present to take pictures for your portfolio and to adjust the lighting cues if necessary.

If you would like to record some moments that are not on the shot list, coordinate them with the director and the Stage Manager ahead of time. Keep in mind that the photographer that is hired to document the production will focus on cast shots and those moments chosen by the director to represent the overall visual realization of the show and you will want to take your own photographs that are representative of your work to include in your portfolio. Everyone wants good photos, but they also want to get through the process as quickly as possible. Costume and scene changes may be required, so the Stage Manager sets up a schedule to proceed through the show, usually in reverse order so that the photo session can start as soon as the audience has cleared the house.

SELECTING PHOTO EQUIPMENT

Taking photos, particularly of the darker scenes, under production conditions is challenging and requires good equipment and practice. Digital cameras have typically not been considered suitable for this, but they are improving and may become the method of choice. Print film has a lower contrast ratio than slide film so slide film has been the medium of choice for lighting designers. Select one that combines high speed with low grain and is balanced for tungsten light (3,200K) rather than a daylight film.

A light meter that you can use to check foot-candle levels onstage when you are setting the lights will also be less prone to being "fooled" than the meter in the camera, and it will come in handy. You will have to interpret the information that you get from both meters, but with experience you will find that you are able to take shots of most of the show "by eye" after consulting the meters for the first few pictures.

PHOTOGRAPHING YOUR WORK

The focus of the photo call tends to be on the actors, but the environment that surrounds them is established through the lighting, and it is a time for you to make a record or your work.

Portfolios that are filled only with Light Plots and paperwork are difficult to evaluate and won't result in much additional work.

Reviews

When the reviews come out, it can be an uplifting or humbling experience for certain individuals and the production as a whole. Theatre reviewers are paid to render opinions about the overall quality of the productions they see. In doing so, they may attribute the relative success, or failure, of a production to an individual or group of individuals. Reviewers are considered to be experts in performance evaluation, but their backgrounds and qualifications vary widely. Most reviewers feel comfortable praising specific performances and noting where improvements might be made in others. Some feel compelled to use half the space of their column to explain the play and then use the rest to give their opinions of the production. Still others begin with a quote from the play and then weave the entire review around this thread.

Whatever the method, it is not uncommon for reviewers to spend a majority of their time writing about the performances and devote a few lines to the other aspects of production. This is partially due to the expectations of the editor and those who buy the paper, but may also be due to the reviewer's hesitancy to write extensively about what are considered to be the "technical areas" of the production. A reviewer does not have to be trained in lighting in order to assess the relative success of the design, but a lack of familiarity with how the technical elements of the production are tied together may inhibit an extended discussion of them in the review. The set will often get a mention, but some reviews are devoid of any remarks about the lighting at all. It's hard not to feel slighted by this, but it is also sometimes regarded as "dodging the bullet" by avoiding a bad review.

When you encounter a "not a word about the lighting" review, it is best to suppose that the reviewer felt that the lighting was well suited to the production and that he or she didn't see any inconsistencies relative to the other production values. When you think about it, this is really what we are striving for. We want the lighting to support the production in such a way that it does not draw attention to itself and befits every moment so well that it is seamlessly joined to the show. If a review does contain some disparaging remarks about the lighting, talk them over with the director and come to an agreement about whether those cues need to be reconsidered for possible changes. Above all remember this: A review, good or bad, is one person's opinion.

Striking the Show

Some productions enjoy long runs that span years and continue through multiple tours. Typical productions have a limited run and may only be performed an average of four to six times for an audience, including matinees.

Striking the show is the final activity that the production staff will undertake together and it requires considerable coordination. In many summer stock situations, planning the **strike** for one show and preparing for the next begins before the first instrument is drawn on the Plot for the opening show of the season. Whatever the circumstances, striking the show is a hectic and dangerous activity and proper planning is essential for the safety of those participating. A meeting with the department heads (sound, electrics, and **carpenters**) to plan out who will occupy the stage and ancillary spaces at various points in the process is definitely in order.

Usually the carpenters will take the stage first to clear the set so that the other crews can have access to the equipment with which they have to work. The exception to this is when there are practicals or sound and lighting cables attached to the set or on the deck. In this case, the electricians should be standing by to remove these items as quickly as possible so that the carpenters can get on with their work. While the carpenters are on the stage, the electricians typically strike the equipment from the Front-of-House positions and begin returning the color and frames to storage. When this task is completed, the stage is usually clear enough that the first electric can be flown in and struck, or it is accessible with a lift or a ladder. The process of clearing and sharing the space continues until all of the equipment and set pieces are struck, stored, returned to stock, or put in the dumpster.

Designers are not always required to participate in the strike, but if you are, work with the crew to overcome any difficulties and coordinate with the other departments to maximize efficiency and keep the work environment safe. Stay focused on the task at hand but also note how the Plot was physically realized in the space and take time to reflect on how this process was unique. Whether you work in that particular venue again or not, there are valuable lessons to be learned and carried on to other projects. It will be hard to forget the things that went wrong, but you also want to remember what went right. Write those things down, keep a list, and refer to it often. It's amazing the things that we learn over and over again simply because we don't have a place to go to remind us of our successes.

Glossary

acting areas – Portions of the stage designated by the lighting designer to enable selective control of the lighting and create a smooth blend of light from fixtures that light the performers. Each acting area is typically eight to ten feet wide and has a focus point at its center.

amp – Short for *ampere*. Unit of measure for electrical current.

angle of incidence – The measure of how far from horizontal a light is, relative to the stage or the subject it is lighting.

apron – The part of the stage platform that protrudes into the audience in front of the proscenium wall.

attribute – (1) Each of the controllable features of a robotic lighting instrument. (2) Part of lighting design software that allows fixture features and accessory designations to be edited for each fixture represented on the Light Plot.

autotransformer – A non–remote dimming device that controls lamp intensity by varying the voltage to the fixture.

backlight – Light that comes from behind an object and is used to separate it from the background.

baffles – Arrangements of metal within a fixture that are used to control the light; particularly to control unwanted spill from exiting the sides or back of the unit.

barn doors – An accessory that fits into the color holder of a lighting fixture and has two or four adjustable leaves to shape the light beam. Typically used on Fresnels.

base – The part of a lamp that connects the lamp assembly to the socket and holds the lamp in a predetermined position relative to the reflector.

batten – Horizontal pipes for hanging curtains, scenery, and lighting instruments. "Dead hung" battens remain in one position; "flown" battens can be raised and lowered.

bi-parting – Curtains that open at the center and travels offstage.

blackout – A transition to darkness that is written with a fade time of zero.

boom – Vertical pipes for hanging lighting instruments.

boomerang – A manual color-changing device used on follow spots.

box boom – Booms that are located at the sides of the audience chamber and occupy the space where box seats used to be located.

border – A wide, short curtain that hangs over the stage to mask the rigging and lighting instruments from the view of the audience.

bump(out) – A lighting cue with a fade time of less than a second.

call – (1) The time when members of the production staff are to report for work. (2) Direction by the Stage Manager to execute a prearranged action.

carpenters – Stagehands who work with scenery and drapery.

centerline – A line that starts at the apron and runs upstage to the back wall, dividing the stage into the left and right segments.

C–clamp – The temporary means of attaching lighting fixtures to battens.

concept – Central idea for the production usually established in the production meeting.

color – Plastic or glass media placed in front of a light to block certain portions of the spectrum.

color reversal – Phenomenon in the human visual system where the exact opposite of a color will be perceived when viewing a particular color is followed by darkness.

color temperature – A measurement, expressed in degrees Kelvin, of the range of the warm (2,800° K) or cool (5,600 K) components of light from a source.

contrast – The relative difference between areas of light and shadow.

contrast ratio – The difference between the darkest and brightest levels that can be differentiated by a type of film, a television camera, or the human eye.

cool – Light that falls into the upper frequency range of the visible spectrum and is perceived as having a significant amount of blue in it.

curtain warmers – Front-of-House lighting that is focused to light the main curtain at those times when it is closed during production.

cyc – Short for *cyclorama*. Traditionally, a curved curtain or backdrop at the back of the stage. Often used interchangeably with the term *sky* today to represent any lightweight muslin curtain that hangs at the back of the stage and is light blue, light gray, or white.

cyc lighting – Strip lights or other fixtures that are used to light the curtain that spans the back of the stage.

donut – A piece of metal with a round hole cut in it, typically about one-half the diameter of the fixture lens, that is placed in the color holder on the front of the ellipsoidal to sharpen the image of a pattern.

drapery – Curtains and soft goods used to dress or mask the stage.

deck – The stage floor.

down light – Lights that are hung directly over the performers. *See also* **top light.**

downstage – Near the front of the stage, close to the audience.

electrics – Locations that are designated for the hanging of lighting fixtures. Electrics usually have circuitry that is connected to the lighting system associated with them.

electrics crew – Stagehands who work with lighting equipment.

envelope – The glass part of a lamp that contains the filament and special gases.

filament – The metal coil in a lamp that glows when an electric current is passed through it.

fill light – The light that fills in the shadows on the side of the face unlit by the key light.

fixture – A stage lighting instrument.

footlights – Lights that are located on the floor at the front of the stage. They are rarely used except for effect.

focus – To point or aim a lighting instrument to a specific place on the stage.

focus call – Time that is set aside for the electricians and the lighting designer to occupy the theatre in order to focus the lights.

focus points – Places on the stage that are designated by the lighting designer as the points where the hottest part of the light should hit. Where the designer stands to adjust the focus of the lights.

foot-candle – Unit of measure for lighting intensity. One foot candle is the amount of light from a candle measured at one foot from the flame.

follow spot – Manually operated lighting instrument used to highlight performers and track their movement about the stage.

front light – Any instrument that lights an object from the front.

gel – Color media that is placed in front of the lens of a lighting fixture to color the light.

gobo – *See* **pattern.**

halogen – Gas that is introduced into the glass envelope of a lamp to prolong filament life.

"the hang" – The time when the lights for a production are put in place and connected to the electrical system.

hair light – The term used for top or backlight in film and television.

high side light – A type of side lighting that is used frequently in traditional productions as well as dance. These instruments may start at the offstage ends of the battens or on pipe-mounted ladders and can continue onstage past the centerline.

instrument – A stage light.

jumper – A short piece of stage cable, usually five feet or less in length.

Kelvin – A scale of degrees used to express the color of light that radiates from a source.

Key – The portion of the Light Plot that shows where designations for unit number, channel assignment, color number, and accessories are placed.

key light – The primary source of light.

ladder – Lighting position where fixtures are hung above one another, but typically not more than two or three across. Resembles a ladder and can be a permanent position (part of the building infrastructure) or hung from the ends of a pipe batten.

lamp – The source of the light in a fixture.

leg – Tall narrow curtains hung at the sides of the stage to mask the audience view into the wings.

lens – Specially formulated glass at the front of a lighting fixture that shapes the light beam and determines its specular qualities.

Lighting Key – A plan view sketch that identifies the light sources and where they are placed relative to the performer.

light ladder – *See* **ladder.**

Light Plot – A plan view of the theatre, drawn to scale, that shows things such as the walls surrounding the stage and audience chamber, the outline of any scenery, the location of the masking, and the lighting instruments on the battens both over the stage and the audience.

Lighting Section – A drawing that represents what we would see if we took a giant saw and cut down through the theatre on the centerline from front to back. The Section is the drawing we look to in order to determine the angle of incidence from the lighting fixtures to the stage.

main curtain – The curtain that closes off the proscenium opening.

Typically made from velour fabric. May be bi–parting, guillotine, or both.

masking – Drapery and flats that are used to limit the view of the audience into the backstage areas or elsewhere.

Master Electrician – Person in charge of the electrics crew.

midstage – The area of the stage that separates upstage and downstage.

negative after-imaging – Phenomenon of the human visual system that occurs in darkness after the eye has been exposed to a lighted scene for a period of time and the light and dark areas of the viewed image are reversed.

non-dim – A stage circuit that is either fully on or off, usually used for operating motors.

op – Short for *operator*; as in board op, spot op, etc.

patch – A method of arranging the circuits in a lighting system to suit each particular production. When computer consoles are used, patching involves assigning the dimmers and their associated circuits to channels in order to create a logical sequence of control groupings.

pattern – A thin sheet of stainless steel that is cut to resemble a specific shape and placed in an ellipsoidal reflector spotlight to project light in that shape.

pipe ends – High side lights that are located only at the offstage ends of the pipes.

plaster line – A line that runs stage left and right between the points at the upstage side of the proscenium opening. The line from which all upstage and downstage measurements are referenced.

practical – A household-style lighting fixture (such as a table lamp, chandelier, or porch light) that is connected to a stage lighting circuit and operated through the lighting console. Practicals are usually outfitted with reduced wattage lamps (10W to 25W) and operated at low intensity so as not to blind the audience.

proscenium (wall) – The wall that separates the stage and the audience chamber. Contains the proscenium opening, through which the audience views the show.

Q – Designation for a cue.

reflector – A shaped polished metal or glass device at the back of a lighting fixture that directs the light output from the lamp to the front of the fixture.

repeater – Intermediate device used in the control of multiple robotic fixtures or accessories.

run crew – The behind-the-scenes staff who work on the production during performances.

shin busters (shins) – Side lighting instruments that are mounted on booms in the wings, primarily used for dance. They are called such because they are mounted with their center at about one foot off the floor and the unwary dancer may incur a shin injury when exiting into the wings.

shutters – Thin stainless steel plates used to shape the light beam in an ellipsoidal reflector spotlight.

side light – Light that strikes an object from the side.

sky (drop) – The flat curtain at the rear of the stage that is generally lit in a way to represent the sky. *See also* **cyc.**

soft goods – Stage curtains, draperies, or backdrops.

special – Any lighting fixture designated for a single or limited purpose.

specular – The quality of light that alludes to the relative "crispness" or "softness" of the light beam.

spike – A temporary mark on the stage floor to indicate the location for a set piece, piece of furniture, or actor.

Stage Manager – The person who organizes and attends rehearsals, coordinates all aspects of the production, is in charge of the production during performance, and calls the cues. Also the communication link between all the facets of the production team during the rehearsal process.

straight in wash – Lighting that covers a broad area of the stage where the fixtures are hung perpendicular to the objects they are lighting.

strike – When all of the temporary construction, sets, lights, sound gear, and all other items used to mount a particular production are removed from the stage after the final performance.

strip light – A metal trough that carries lamps and reflectors spaced closely together with provisions for glass roundels or plastic color media in a hinged cover. Provides an even wash of light and is typically used to light a cyc or sky drop.

teaser – A border that hangs just downstage of the main curtain that is made from the same material, usually velour, as the main curtain.

throw distance – The distance from the lighting instrument to the object it is lighting. This measurement is derived from the Lighting Section drawing.

top hat – An accessory that fits into the color holder of a lighting instrument to control light scatter (halation) from a lighting instrument. Typically used on ellipsoidals, especially those in Front–of–House positions.

top light – Lights that are hung directly over the performers. *See also* **down light.**

tormentor – The legs that hang at the front of the stage, are made of the same material as the front curtain, and match it in color.

traveler – Any curtain that operates on a track.

trim height – The optimum height for the flown electrics, taking into account scenery, masking, and focus points. Trim height is determined through the Lighting Section drawing and is indicated on the Light Plot.

unit – Designation for a stage lighting fixture. Usually refers to the numbered fixture position on a batten.

uplight – Light that emanates from below the object being lit.

upstage – Toward the back of the stage, away from the audience.

valance – Drapery that hangs at the front of the stage and is made from the same material as the main curtain. Generally, a more ornamental form of a teaser.

value – The relative darkness or lightness of a color.

voltage – The measurement of electrical potential relative to a zero point.

warm – Light that falls into the lower frequency range of the visible spectrum and is perceived as having a significant amount of red or yellow in it.

wash – Even coverage of light over a broad area.

wattage – The measurement of electrical power (Volts x Amps).

wings – The sides of the stage outside the performance area that are masked from the view of the audience by scenery or the legs of a drapery set.

x-ray – An archaic term for strip lights used to light a cyc or sky.

yoke – Flat metal band in the shape of a U that connects the lighting fixture to the C–clamp and allows tilt adjustments to be made to the light.

Z-rack – A portable rack used for hanging and transporting costumes.

Index

About the Author

Charles I. Swift brings nearly three decades of experience to his work as a lighting designer, educator, and theatre consultant. Mr. Swift has designed a wide range of productions and worked in various capacities on production teams throughout the United States. He has brought his skills to bear in implementing technical systems in theatres the world over and is currently engaged in designing systems for a variety of venues throughout the Southeast.

Mr. Swift is an Associate Member of the American Society of Theatre Consultants (ASTC), a member of the Illuminating Engineering Society of North America (IESNA), the United States Institute for Theatre Technology (U.S.I.T.T.), and maintains membership in the International Alliance of Theatrical Stage Employees (IATSE).

He received his B.S. in Design and Production (summa cum laude) from the State University of New York at New Paltz and earned an M.F.A. in Scene and Lighting Design from Carnegie Mellon University.

Mr. Swift has taught stagecraft and lighting design in the State University System of New York and is currently an adjunct theatre faculty member in the College of the Arts at Kennesaw State University.